5400 00126 075

D0745322

REINVENTING CANADA

ANTHONY WESTELL

DUNDURN PRESS
TORONTO & OXFORD

Editor: Doris Cowan
Printed and bound in Canada by Webcom

The publisher wishes to acknowledge the generous assistance and ongoing support of the **Canada Council,**
the **Book Publishing Industry Development Program** of the **Department of Canadian Heritage,** the
Ontario Arts Council, the **Ontario Publishing Centre** of the **Ministry of Culture, Tourism and
Recreation,** and the **Ontario Heritage Foundation.**

Care has been taken to trace the ownership of copyright material used in the text. The author and
publisher welcome any information enabling them to rectify any reference or credit in subsequent editions.

J. Kirk Howard, Publisher

Canadian Cataloguing in Publication Data

Westell Anthony, 1926–
          Reinventing Canada

(Towards the new millennium)
ISBN 1-55002-228-8

1. Canada – Politics and government – 1993– .*
2. Nationalism – Canada. 3. Federal government –
Canada. I. Title. II. Series.

FC635.W47 1994   971.064'7   C94-932134-6
F1034.2.W47 1994

Dundurn Press Limited	Dundurn Distribution	Dundurn Press Limited
2181 Queen Street East	73 Lime Walk	1823 Maryland Avenue
Suite 301	Headington, Oxford	P.O. Box 1000
Toronto, Canada	England	Niagara Falls, N.Y.
M4E 1E5	0X3 7AD	U.S.A. 14302-1000

FOREWORD

by Eric Malling
Host of CTV's "W-5" Program

Tony Westell's problem as a journalist, to put this in a backhand way, is that he thinks too much. But it's never the conventional way of thinking. When we worked together for the *Toronto Star* in Ottawa – he as the national affairs columnist and I as a junior reporter – I watched him turn story after story on its ear. If the entire Parliamentary Press Gallery was chasing the same scandal or scoundrel, he was as likely as not to take the other side and ask, "What's so bad here?" – or argue conversely, "What's really bad here no one is reporting."

In the 1970s when the conventional wisdom was that Prime Minister Trudeau had the only answer to the national unity problem Westell came to the opposite conclusion in his book *Paradox: Trudeau as Prime Minister*. He was right. Twenty years later, Quebec separatism is very much alive. During the FLQ terrorist crisis in 1970, when other respected Ottawa commentators saw the imposition of the War Measures Act as a plot against democracy, Westell argued that the cabinet had simply been bumbling. Current accounts attest that in fact ministers didn't know what else to do.

In 1975, when Trudeau talked in a year-end interview about a "new society," most reporters fuelled fears about his radical intent. Westell published a book called *The New Society* in which he argued that Trudeau had not gone far enough, and his prescriptions for more citizen involvement, an overhaul of Parliament, and a whole new definition of work are today part of mainstream debate.

When his newspaper, the *Star*, had daily fits over foreign control of the economy, Westell was writing about the international economy. Long before free trade was proposed or debated, he saw it as inevitable. And whatever he thinks of so-called investigative reporting today – I prefer to call it enterprise reporting – Westell invented it in this country when, during the 1965 election campaign, he took to reporting in quotation remarks what Opposition leader John Diefenbaker was saying and then following with the facts in brackets. Mike Lavoie, our colleague on the *Star* and now senior producer at "W-5," says that when a reporter hears the phrase "sacred cow" he should think of 600 pounds of pot roast. We both learnt that from Tony.

Conventional wisdom today says that constitutional problems will disappear if we can get the economy perking. In this book Westell, true to form, argues the opposite. Look at our debt, look at our deficits. Every penny the federal government spends on its own operations, every wage and other bill it pays, is borrowed money. We obviously can't afford to buy national unity. We can't afford the traditional glue of Confederation – "Since you've done something dumb for him, now you have to do something dumb for me."

Conventional wisdom says that Canada is a rich country and its problems can be blamed on incompetent politicians. Westell argues that Canada's wealth may have been a temporary, postwar blip, and that the very structure of the country makes it ungovernable in all but the best of times. To think in different terms, perhaps we can't afford both Ottawa and the provinces. Perhaps big countries cobbled together in the nineteenth century are by nature too inefficient for today's international economy. To end the bickering, why not sovereignty-association for every region?

Conventional wisdom of the left blames a conservative corporate agenda for our economic troubles. On the right, it's the welfare state and its entitlement mentality. Westell demolishes the cant on both sides. Historically, left and right haven't mattered much in Canadian government, and today they may be irrelevant. How else can you explain Saskatchewan Premier Roy Romanow having to step into a cold fiscal shower after the binge of Grant Devine's Conservatives? Perhaps the new spectrum – the new populism Westell predicts – will see practical people who make things work, with their hands or their heads, aligned against those who deal only with perfection in process – the interest groups, the bureaucrats, the lawyers and, too often, crusading journalists.

In my opinion the most important contribution Westell makes is in challenging, or goading, us to rethink the political and media agenda which has recently been dominated by the trivial. Every slight is racism or sexism. Every environmental problem or difficulty becomes a catastrophe. Every government program is now an absolute entitlement. Even modest changes in the way we are governed are threatening. We're a family in trouble. We've become obsessed with the trivial because we don't want to face real problems. Our standard of living is falling, we're too deeply in debt, and our country doesn't work very well anymore.

This book is a contribution to facing those problems, and it starts on solutions. The late Borden Spears wrote that at best journalists help prepare people for change. *Reinventing Canada* does just that.

ACKNOWLEDGMENTS

I began this book in 1987 when I took sabbatical leave from Carleton University to research and write about the future of socialism – if it had one. If socialism was in fact dying, done in by triumphant capitalism, I wanted to know whether some new alternative to capitalism would arise to replace it, or if indeed we were at the "end of history." So, being a journalist rather than a scholar, I asked a lot of experts, in both North America and Europe, to all of whom I am grateful. I also read up on socialism, and after seven or eight months – a long time for a journalist to work on a story – I thought I had the questions answered. Just to finish up, I popped into the New York Public Library to check a few references. A month or two later, I came out with a whole new set of ideas.

By the time I returned to Carleton I had begun to write. However, it was my turn to be an academic administrator, or rather, an administrator of academics, and in my experience there is something about administration that dries up the creative juices. Perhaps it is the fact that there are almost daily crises demanding your full attention, and even when there is no crisis, you know one will erupt at any moment, so starting other work seems pointless. I didn't get much writing done in those years, but I was thinking about my subject, watching the world change, and becoming more and more concerned about Canada's inability to deal with its problems.

A community of scholars and demanding students is an excellent place in which to hone ideas. I began to apply my analysis of the struggle between socialism and capitalism to an understanding – perhaps I should call it an interpretation – of the Canadian crisis. When I retired I was able to resume serious writing, and this book is the result. I owe it to Carleton, but Carleton of course bears no responsibility for my ideas. In fact, I can't think of a person there who would fully agree with what I have to say.

I am grateful also to my friend Eric Malling, the only TV journalist I know who succeeds in turning ideas into immensely popular programs. He shared ideas with me, read my manuscript, suggested improvements that I at once adopted, and spread the word that I had something that might be worth publishing. A friend indeed ...

In 1977 I published a book called *The New Society*. It sold modestly and has long been out of print, but I've been told more than once that it was not without influence in its time. If anyone now remembers it and reads this book, they may recognize some arguments, notably in the section on federalism. But the greater part of the analysis here – the context in which ideas appear – is entirely new, and as far as I know, unique.

Introduction
A NEW POPULISM

Realizing that large numbers of Canadians were worried about the future of their country and deeply mistrustful of their political leadership, Prime Minister Brian Mulroney in 1990 appointed the Citizens' Forum on Canada's Future, allegedly to get ideas on how to put things right. As he gave the Forum commissioners the absurdly short time of eight months to do the job, it was probably never intended to be much more than a public relations gimmick. But under the energetic leadership of Keith Spicer, formerly a journalist and now chairman of the Canadian Radio-television and Communications Commission, the members of the Forum did manage to involve several hundred thousand people in a dialogue about Canada's problems. They learned enough about the mood of the people to say in their report, published in 1991: "Canada is in a crisis. This is a crisis identified and experienced by the people of Canada as immediately as a drought affects a farmer. This is a crisis of identity, a crisis of understanding, a crisis of leadership. We have arrived at this conclusion not because participants used the word crisis – few of them did – but because what they told us adds up, mercilessly, to this conclusion."

The Forum commissioners conceded that many of those who participated in the discussion groups were ill informed on the problems they discussed and that many groups in fact reached no conclusions. When participants did express opinions, there was no way of knowing whether they were representative of the population generally. But a dialogue had begun, and the commissioners urged the Mulroney government to "encourage and enrich it" in the process of "national rebuilding" – in itself an interesting conclusion with its implicit message that Canada needed to be rebuilt. Mulroney did not act on their advice, probably because he thought the federal and provincial governments could work out the problems themselves without further input from the people. This they quickly attempted to do, producing the package of constitutional reforms that became known as the Charlottetown accord.

If Mulroney ever actually read his commissioners' report, he had apparently missed a key finding. When Canadians gave their views on the country's political institutions and leadership, close to 100 percent of their comments were negative. They didn't trust their politicians, the political system, or indeed the mass media, which in their view often made a bad situation worse. "Obviously," said the commissioners, "there is a need for the political system to respond better. That need is at the heart of our country's problems" – another provocative conclusion.

The report finished with the warning that "no hyperbole or political hedge can screen any member of any legislature who thwarts the will of the people on this matter. The voters are watching and waiting." How true that was! When the federal and political leadership, backed by business, labour, and most of the media, submitted the Charlottetown accord to the people in a referendum, the people's answer was no. And when the Conservatives called an election in 1993, the voters threw them not only out of office but almost entirely out of the House of Commons. In the most astonishing election in Canadian history more than 30 percent voted for two new parties proposing radical change, the Bloc Québécois and Reform. The commissioners' warnings about the public mood and the retribution awaiting politicians who failed to recognize and act upon it were fully confirmed.

One reason for the disaffection, obviously, was the economic condition of the country – that is to say, the inability of the government to bring back the good times of full employment and rising incomes. But there is something deeper that is unsettling society, not only in Canada, but in most Western democracies. Nothing seems to work well any more and there is a sense that we are at a turning point in history, with leaders who are just as lost as we are. The old ideologies of left and right are irrelevant, and the centre, while crowded, does not hold. Our parliaments no longer represent us. To refer to someone as an "official," once a term of respect, is now abuse. Official policies seldom work and official explanations are often wrong, and sometimes lies. Religion is of little help: the "official" God is either dead or has lost interest, and his priests turn out to be no better than the rest of us, too often they are worse. Beggars line our streets, and the homeless sleep on warm air vents if they are lucky. Big Business and Big Labour seem to be interested only in the bottom line, which is their own welfare. Too many of our kids can't read or write well. Our jobs are not secure. The environment, even the sun, is threatening. Shopping is not as much fun as it used to be, because there is the nagging suspicion that consuming more goods and services won't make us happier. So we turn restlessly towards new parties, or new leaders of old parties, or protest movements, but usually we find demagogues or do-gooders with slogan solutions too simple to be sensible. It's a world off the rails and we aren't going to put up with it any more. Or we won't put up with it if we can just figure out who's to blame and how to put things right.

There is everywhere – as the Forum commissioners discovered – a demand for a new sort of politics, politics that work. Let's call it a "New Populism." Now, populism is one of those tricky words that change their meaning over time and in different countries. Populist parties in Russia and the United States in the last century arose in response to different problems and proposed different solutions. There have been several attempts at populism in Canada, some originating on the political right and some on the left. Nowadays journalists often use "populist" to describe a politician who seems to be popular, but that's just sloppy use of the word. A common thread running through the history of populism, which separates it from other political movements, is that it arises as a reaction against rapid change in society. At its core is the suspicion that a few are forcing change on the many, and while the few are profiting, the many are suffering. In the past the many were peasants or farmers, and the few they blamed for their problems tended to be landowners, bankers, railway tycoons, grain dealers, etc. Now the many are all those who feel threatened by economic and social change because they live in remote regions or dying towns, far from the centres of power, or work in declining industries or minimum-wage jobs. The few they mistrust are Big Government, or sometimes Big Labour, Big Business, or Big Media.

The populist plan is usually to oust the elites and rely for leadership on "the will of the people" as expressed in some form of direct democracy – for example, plebiscites. But, paradoxically, populist movements often throw up charismatic and autocratic leaders. There may also be some fairly simple economic cure-all, such as slashing government spending to balance the budget, or cutting immigration to keep out foreigners. Ross Perot, the charismatic billionaire businessman, tapped the huge reservoir of populist sentiment in the 1992 U.S. presidential election campaign with his plan to cut spending, cancel free trade with Mexico, and consult the people by way of televised town hall meetings across the country. In Canada, the Reform party did well in the election by promising to slash social spending and thus balance the budget in three years, and to submit major issues to the people in referendums.

For now, with more detail to be filled in later, we'll define our New Populism as an impatient desire by ordinary people to regain from the few (hapless politicians and bungling bureaucrats) effective control of a society that seems to be running out of control and downhill. This book contains some New Populist ideas about regaining control and putting things right. But unlike the old populisms it offers no easy certainties or swift cure-alls. The problems are profound, and the search for solutions is made more difficult by the fact that the world keeps changing. There are certainly no solutions that will take us back to the comfortable optimism of the 1950s and '60s, or to the flatulent prosperity of the 1980s. When so much depends on what happens elsewhere in the world, we have only limited control over our future. But we can position ourselves to make the best of whatever the world offers – if we have the courage to question the basic assumptions on which we have built our economic and political lives, revise some and discard those that no longer work. Reworking the margins of our system of government by adding bits and pieces to the constitution, changing the rules of parliamentary procedure, holding more referendums, or restructuring social programs won't get at the roots of our problems. Nor is it reasonable to insist that we must return to a freebooting capitalism in which the strong and privileged flourish and the weak and unlucky go into the social garbage. We have to discover the real problems that underlie our discontents, and find real solutions that serve the entire community.

There are those who say that now, in 1994, with a new Liberal government in power and the economy apparently improving, the national mood is better and no radical reforms are necessary. That seems to be the view of Prime Minister Jean Chrétien, who keeps saying that he was elected to fix the economy, not to talk about the constitution. Like a lot of people, he assumes they are separate problems – but they aren't. Government plays an enormous role in the modern economy, and when the system of government is failing – as the Citizens' Forum found it was – the economy is bound to be in trouble. It's past time to resume the dialogue the Forum began and, this time, to dig deeper into the fundamental problems. That's the purpose of this book.

Our social, economic, and political systems have been evolving in the Western democracies for hundreds of years, and we take a lot of basic ideas for granted – some of which turn out on examination to be myths. Before making changes we need to take a clear-eyed look at where we are, and this is the task in Chapter 1. In Chapter 2 we discover why the systems that worked so well in the past are now misfiring in most democracies, and why we have to make wrenching changes in consciousness if we are to survive in the changing world. Chapter 3, "The Canadian Sickness," shows why the general malaise is more serious in Canada than in most countries: it's because the central values that have defined our national identity and justified our national independence are threatened by forces seemingly beyond our control.

Having analysed our problems in terms that will surprise, shock, even outrage many Canadians, we turn to solutions. First we ask, in Chapter 4, whether our institutions – our system of federalism and our parliamentary form of government – are part of the problem or part of the solution. The Forum commissioners were told they're a problem; they are, and this chapter outlines why. In Chapter 5 we ask, What's to be done? Don't expect pat answers. Fundamental changes will work only if they arise from public debate and have majority support – that's New Populism – so we can't presume to dictate solutions to our problems. We can and do, however, frame the hard questions Canadians must address if they want to master their national future. For starters, Is Canada as we know it a viable country? If not, what are our options? And how do we force the complacent politicians to respond to our concerns?

As this book goes to press, a government committed to separation has been elected in Quebec. The worst response in the rest of Canada would be to take the bloody-minded attitude that because Quebec seeks change in the organization of the country, no changes will be allowed. The best response would be to see the election of the Parti Québécois as a challenge and an opportunity to make changes that will improve the way the country works for all provinces. If we are not willing now to "reinvent Canada," Quebec may well do it for us.

CHAPTER ONE

How We Got Here

To set a course into the future, we have first to understand where we are now, and how we got here. We have to learn from history, and right away we have a problem. Does history in fact have lessons to teach, or was the past just a series of accidents? Was there some pattern to events, or was it a matter of chance whether events went one way or another? In Europe and North America in the last century, the consensus among those who worried about such things was that we were in an age of progress, with civilization becoming steadily more civilized and the human condition improving. The view from the end of the twentieth century is very different. After two world wars of unparalleled ferocity, the invention of weapons that threaten human survival, and now, in our greed for material wealth, the erosion of the environment on which life itself depends, can we still believe in progress? Perhaps the religious fundamentalists are right when they warn that we are at the mercy of an implacable God who is taking revenge on a world that won't listen and obey; or possibly Darwin's process of natural selection is eliminating the human species, allowing the globe to pass to a new species able to survive in the environment we have created. Or maybe it all depends on accidents of birth: remarkable individuals who appear and shape events for good or ill. Would we have had a Second World War if Hitler had not been born, or won it without Churchill, Roosevelt, and Stalin? We cannot know the answers, but if we accept the view that our fate is not ours to shape, there is little point in striving to make the future better. If that is your view, read no further. The New Populism is based on the idea that progress is at least possible, and that it is our responsibility to learn from the past and to make the future better.

One way to think about the past and the possibilities of the future is to use the Hegelian dialectic, a form of analytical dialogue. Georg Wilhelm Friedrich Hegel (1770–1831) was a German philosopher and seminal thinker, and other philosophers have been arguing for a century or so about what he meant and whether he was right. I do not intend to enter that debate, but Hegel's ideas on progress, applied in the most uncomplicated form, provide a way to organize knowledge of the past, and perhaps to peek into the future. He saw history as the story of the human race rising gradually through higher and higher levels of consciousness until we finally achieve complete fulfilment in perfect freedom. The level of consciousness determines the type of social organization, and the level is raised by the clash of ideas and beliefs – not merely political debate as we know it, but the clash of whole cultures and social systems. The prevailing vision of the world, called a *thesis*, is contradicted by another, the *antithesis*. In the ensuing struggle both visions are shown to be flawed. But they influence each other and the outcome is not the triumph of one over the other, but a *synthesis* of the two. This new and higher level of consciousness becomes the new thesis. With fewer flaws, it gives rise to a new and better social order, but it in turn is contradicted, leading to a new and still higher synthesis. Finally, all contradictions will be resolved and the perfect society will be in place. The dialectic will end and so, in that sense, will history. But we aren't there yet.

Using this theory of how change and progress occur, we can think of the history of Europe in the period roughly between 1750 and 1850 as a clash between the prevailing thesis of feudal society contradicted by the antithesis of a new society emerging from the Industrial Revolution. In this vast process a new class of men of business challenged the landed aristocracy, democratic ideas battled with conservative autocracy, and scientific and humanist values undermined traditional religion. The synthesis was an early version of capitalist society. That is to say, the owners of the means of production – mines, mills, factories, railroads, banks, and so on – became a new ruling class in a fledgling political democracy. The aristocracy survived in most countries by parlaying their lands into industrial capital and a seat on the board of directors of the new corporations. In government, parliaments elected by the middle classes became partners – usually senior partners – with the former rulers, kings and queens, and their courts of aristocratic advisers. The churches lost much of their political power but remained influential in setting moral standards.

When we read about the industrial labourers – men, women, and children – in early capitalist society slaving in grimy factories in squalid cities, it is easy to say that they might have been better off to remain peasants in feudal society, even accepting that the countryside was in many respects a vast rural slum. It may indeed be that what industrial workers gained in the short run in wages and opportunity they lost in quality of life rooted in traditional communities, rural skills, and religious values. But when early capitalist society became the thesis, a new antithesis, socialism, arose to expose its internal contradictions. And the struggle between capitalist and socialist ideas – on what motivates human beings and how society can best be organized – has been driving the dialectic of progress in the industrialized nations of the West and beyond for more than a century. But as soon as we mention the terms capitalism and socialism we must examine what we mean by them. Like the word populism, they are tossed around in everyday political discussion but seldom defined; in fact, there are no universally accepted definitions and, to avoid confusion, it is important to explain the sense in which they are used here.

THE THESIS: CAPITALISM

Capitalism is an economic system in which the means of production, distribution, and exchange are privately owned, and capital, labour, goods, and services are traded in free markets. Obviously, private ownership of property and some degree of private enterprise in commerce have existed almost since history began, but prior to the Industrial Revolution most economic activities were subject to arbitrary rules and regulations laid down by the king or the bishop or some other ruler. Workers were bound to the owners of the land on which they laboured, craftsmen were controlled by their guilds, and permission from on high was required to operate even a town market. Rather than free-market economies, therefore, they were in some measure command economies – that is to say, always subject to some autocratic controller. A number of factors combined to change this age-old system in Europe. Historians differ on what happened first and on which factors were most important, and for our purpose it will be sufficient to illustrate the complexity of the process by mentioning only a few facts and ideas, and those in briefest outline. The Reformation in the sixteenth century gave rise to Protestantism, which more than Roman Catholicism encouraged the emergence of the rational, self-directed, responsible individual and the scientific method of inquiry. This in turn generated individual enterprise and an explosion of new technologies – ways to produce things more cheaply – which eventually replaced traditional crafts with machines in urban factories. Large pools of capital had to be organized to finance the new industries, requiring a new financial services industry. Another factor seems to have been the way in which British landowners ruthlessly drove peasants from their holdings to make way for more profitable sheep, and thus created a class of labourers hiring themselves out for work in the new cities. In continental Europe treasure from the New World upset traditional rural economies and created a class of merchants who rose in power at the expense of aristocratic landowners.

With the rapid expansion of economic activity the new class of capitalists adopted democratic forms and ideas, in part no doubt to gain political power and protect themselves from interference by royal governments and feudal aristocrats. This is not to say that the emerging capitalists always favoured full democracy and equal opportunity in a free market. Rather, they wanted to manage commercial and political affairs to suit their own ends. Karl Marx was not entirely wrong when he derided cabinets in parliamentary democracies as the executive committees of the bourgeoisie, or capitalists.

Adam Smith, the great British economist who first described the workings of a market system in *The Wealth of Nations* (1776) and has since become the patron saint of capitalism, had few illusions about businessmen. They were motivated only by self-interest, but competition in a free market would guide them (as if by an Invisible Hand, in Smith's graphic metaphor) to serve the public interest. To invent an example, although a baker might be interested only in selling bread at the highest possible price to make a fat profit, the market would ensure a supply of loaves at reasonable prices to meet public demand. It would do this because when the demand for bread was greater than the supply, prices would rise as customers competed for the available loaves, yielding the first baker his enviable profits. Then other bakers would open for business, to bake more bread and get a share of the profits. With a greater supply, prices would fall and consumers would benefit. Or to use another example, a merchant might prosper for a time by selling shoddy goods at high prices, but others would see how well he was doing and enter the market to compete by selling better quality for less. Thus competition would ensure that the consumer got the best value for money, without the king or the bishop issuing a single order.

In a similar way, the market would also manage the supply of work and the rates of pay. When there were more workers than jobs available, wages would fall, and as labour became less expensive, businessmen would hire more workers for new enterprises. When there were more jobs than workers to fill them, employers would compete to hire by offering higher wages and drawing new labour into the market, until the supply of work and demand for labour were in balance. Smith realized that instead of competing fairly, thus allowing the Invisible Hand its wonders to perform, businessmen would conspire to profit by limiting competition and fixing prices, or by agreeing in private to hold down wages, or by persuading government to make laws limiting competition. For this reason he was suspicious of any attempt by government to regulate markets, arguing that it would almost always be best to leave them alone and rely on competition to bring supply into balance with demand at a fair price – that is, to adopt (in the familiar French phrase) a policy of laissez-faire.

A problem with this thesis is that while markets may be rational, people often aren't – and that includes our most respected and successful capitalists. From time to time people rush to buy or sell for quite irrational reasons, creating a destructive cycle of boom and bust. Markets are without doubt efficient in regulating economic activity over time, but in the short term they can impose hardship on those who least deserve it, the people without resources to ride out the busts. In short, markets are not concerned with justice and in some degree are incompatible with political democracy, which seeks justice for all.

A more familiar criticism of capitalism has been that it is driven by private greed and is therefore essentially immoral. Greed for profit certainly enters into it, but greed was not invented by capitalists and is only one among many motives for economic enterprise. Long before capitalism, some people in every society – and perhaps every person in his or her heart – desired to become rich and powerful, to explore and invent, to conquer, and to be honoured by their fellows – in short, to leave their mark upon the world. War and politics, either secular or religious, were usually the means to success in feudal societies. But capitalism channels these restless human energies into economic activity, and also accommodates the demand for dynamic change that is a feature of the modern world. A more telling criticism of capitalism is that it dehumanizes workers by treating them as mere factors of production, like oil or steel or any other material, to be hired or discarded in a market in which as individuals they have little bargaining power.

The justification of capitalism has usually been that while it may be immoral in theory and unfair in distributing the wealth it nevertheless delivers more goods to more people than any other economic system. More recently, there have been attempts to give capitalism intellectual coherence and respectability, notably with the argument that by dispersing power instead of centralizing it in the hands of the government it promotes freedom and democracy. For example, Michael Novak, the U.S. conservative thinker, has argued that while capitalism can flourish without democracy, as it does in some authoritarian countries, it is difficult to build democracy without capitalism.

THE ANTITHESIS: SOCIALISM

If capitalism is a system without an inspiring vision, socialism is a vision of a glorious destination without a map for getting there. It is much misunderstood, not least by those who claim to be socialists. Many, perhaps most, Canadians identify it in domestic politics with government control of almost everything, and abroad with cruel, corrupt, and incompetent regimes, notably in the former Soviet Union. More generally, socialism in the West is associated with well-meaning but bumbling bureaucracies and greedy trade unions, both of them out of touch with economic realities. Certainly there have been governments which called themselves socialist and were cruel or bumbling, or both, just as there have been governments which called themselves capitalist and were cruel or incompetent, or both. And trade unions, while claiming to be progressive, often appear determined to conserve the recent past, in which their members flourished, without much regard for new realities and the interests of other groups.

"Socialism," then, is a word that has been used in widely different senses. But one has only to dip into the vast literature on the history of socialist thought to understand that it has always been more a cry for freedom, democracy, and social justice than a coherent ideology with a political program. It is no accident at all that many socialist leaders were also clergymen. They saw socialism as a way to put their religion into practice, a system of ideas morally superior to the capitalism in which they lived. The values of socialism are those of the French Revolution: liberty, equality, fraternity.

According to *A History of European Socialism,* by the U.S. historian Albert S. Lindemann (Yale University Press, 1984), the word "socialist" was first widely used in the 1830s to stress man's social and co-operative nature in opposition to the competitive individualism fostered by emerging capitalism. Some early socialists were utopians, seeking to turn back the Industrial Revolution and create model communities of farmers and craftsmen. Others believed that industrialization, properly managed, could create a world of plenty in which people would be freed from the need to compete for scarce resources – food, housing, warmth, and the other essentials – and could live in peace and harmony.

In his book *Before Marx: Socialism and Communism in France, 1830–48* (Macmillan Press, London, 1983), Paul E. Corcoran says:

> Such a [socialist] perspective meant that one must reject the idea that crime, violence, unemployment, poverty, broken homes, prostitution and high infant mortality resulted from sin and individual moral culpability. It meant rejecting an economic system based upon private property, unlimited competition, avarice and a laissez-faire attitude toward unemployment, starvation wages and crushing working conditions for women and children. It meant rejecting a Church which taught inequality, submission and quiescence while granting a seal of legitimacy to tyrannical governments. It meant rejecting a political regime based upon inherited or bought privilege and corrupt administration, a regime which was unable to represent the people and unwilling to take responsibility for their moral, intellectual and physical well-being.

Emile Durkheim (1858–1917), an eminent French sociologist, studied the history of socialist thought and produced a careful definition of what constituted socialism and what did not. (See *Socialism and Saint-Simon,* edited by Alvin Gouldner, Antioch Press, 1958.) Preparing a series of lectures, he wrote: "Socialism is not a science, a sociology in miniature – it is a cry of grief, sometimes of anger, uttered by men who feel most keenly our collective malaise."

Socialists, he said, believed that poor workers lacked the power to bargain on equal terms with wealthy capitalists to whom they sold their labour. Thus they were compelled to work for less than their true value. Socialists, therefore, wanted to get the state involved in economic affairs as a counterbalance to capital. It was not their wish to subordinate economics to politics, but rather to move economics out of the private sector and into a major role, perhaps even the most important role, in public affairs. Nor did they wish to abolish private wealth, but to interest the state in the means by which industry and commerce produced wealth. But Durkheim perceived that socialism was more than a matter of economic struggle, and he described its interests in terms that would still serve: "For example, they [socialists] are understood generally – at least today – to demand a more democratic organization of society, more liberty in marriage relations, juridical equality of the sexes, a more altruistic morality, a simplification of legal processes, etc."

Fenner Brockway, a British Labour MP and later Lord Brockway, wrote in *Britain's First Socialists: The Levellers, Agitators and Diggers of the English Revolution* (Quartet Books, London, 1980):

> The opponents of socialism often identify it with state authoritarianism. That is emphatically not true. Karl Marx looked forward to the withering away of the state, though he justified the dictatorship of the proletariat during the transition from capitalism to communism. Unhappily, "communist" states have used a prolonged transition to suppress freedom of expression, but democratic socialists passionately believe that liberty of thought is the necessary condition for progress and the realization of truth.

Although a revolutionary Marxist leader in Germany, before she was murdered in 1919 Rosa Luxemburg warned that the Russian style of communism could easily end in dictatorship, and she is said to have coined the aphorism "Socialism without democracy is not socialism."

In *The Left in Europe Since 1789* (World University Library, McGraw-Hill), David Caute summarized the beliefs of "The Left Today":

> Popular sovereignty signifies at least the *liberty* to a voice in public affairs, to a share in the control of one's destiny; the *equality* of men in so far as they all enjoy this liberty and are likely to use it to achieve a wider measure of social and economic equality; a certain *optimism* about men's ability to govern themselves; *rationalism* in the sense that it denies metaphysically derived sources of authority such as Divine Right; *anti-militarism* by analogy, for if the people of one nation can

attain sufficient harmony to distribute sovereignty among themselves, then surely the different nations can also learn to regulate their differences peacefully; *sympathy for the oppressed* in so far as it puts them within reach of changing their own condition; *social reform* because a sovereign people could hardly avoid reforming the society over which they had previously not been sovereign and because the long-term effect of the totality of social reforms is, whatever their intention, to increase popular sovereignty; and finally *movement* because this insistent demand has proved to be the most dynamic force for change in modern European history.

But if socialism is such a beneficent vision, how has it acquired such a bad name? Part of the answer has been relentless anti-socialist propaganda by capitalists who feared for their own power and wealth and, conveniently, controlled most of the mass media. Few daily papers in the Western democracies have had a good word to say for socialism. A favourite villain has been Karl Marx, now perceived by many as a sort of Demon King who invented the Evil Empire, as President Reagan called the former Soviet Union. That is completely wrong. Marx was hardly a pleasant person but, as with all other socialists, his goal was the liberation of man. To gain that end, he thought that revolution against the capitalist class would be necessary, although he seems not to have completely ruled out the idea that democracy might make possible a revolution without violence. Like Hegel, Marx believed that progress occurred as the result of a dialectic between opposing forces, but he argued that Hegel had got it upside down. Indeed, he claimed to have stood Hegel on his head by showing that "it's not the consciousness of men which determines their existence, it is on the contrary their social existence which determines their consciousness."

In his dialectic, each succeeding form of society was ruled by the class that owned the means of production and was able, therefore, to create a legal, political, and cultural superstructure – a consciousness – to serve its purposes. Change occurred when the ruling class was overthrown by those it exploited, who then created their own society. In other words, it was not the evolution of consciousness that determined social organization, but revolutionary change in social organization that changed consciousness. Marx saw the rise of capitalism and its ability to generate wealth as a necessary step in this historical process. But he saw also the way in which early capitalists exploited their workers, treating their labour as just another factor in production, to be hired as cheaply as possible and worked as hard as possible. This created two classes, those who survived by selling their labour for wages and those who owned the means of production or prospered by owning capital which they lent to others for interest. Eventually, he insisted, as capital was concentrated in fewer and fewer hands and the conditions of the workers – the proletariat – became intolerable, the workers would over-throw the capitalists and establish a socialist society which would pave the way for communism.

Under socialism, the working-class majority would seize control of the state and use state power to end capitalism by taking the means of production into public ownership. The workers would thereby establish a productive and classless society in which there would be plenty for all. As co-operation replaced competition and every individual could develop to maximum poten-tial, communism would emerge. There would be no need for a state to regu-late and police the new society of new people, in which the governing princi-ple would be "From each according to his ability, to each according to his need." Thus Marx's dialectic, like Hegel's, would end in a Utopia. As he explained it in *The Communist Manifesto,* which he wrote in 1848 with his friend and collaborator, Friedrich Engels: "In place of the old bourgeois soci-ety, with its classes and class antagonisms, we shall have an association in which the free development of each is the condition for the free development of all." This is undeniably a noble vision, and it is interesting to note in pass-ing that many of the practical political means to a socialist society set out in the famous manifesto have long since been adopted in whole or in part in democratic countries: "A heavy progressive or graduated income tax ... Centralization of credit in the hands of the state by means of a national bank ... Extension of factories and instruments of production owned by the state ... Equal obligation of all to work ... Free education for all children in public schools ... Abolition of children's factory labour," etc.

Incidentally, it is wrong to think that the collapse of communism in the Soviet Union has disproved once and for all Marx's version of the dialectic. In his theory it was necessary for society to progress through capitalism and achieve the potential for material abundance before it could move on to socialism. His impatient followers tried to take a shortcut to socialism when Russia was still in the early stages of capitalism, with much of it more or less a feudal society. Marx would probably not be at all surprised at their failure, and might point out that Russia is now trying to develop a capitalist system – in other words, it is back at an earlier and necessary stage of his dialectic, with socialism still waiting in the wings.

Nevertheless, Marx and his followers were the source of bitter division, which weakened the international socialist movement and aided its enemies. Because Marx thought he had discovered the process by which progress occurred, he argued that his socialism was scientific and all other forms no better than Utopian dreaming – or, even worse, the treason of middle-class democrats who professed to be socialists but in the practice of parliamentary politics actually protected the right of capital to exploit the workers. His opponents in the socialist movement accepted much of his analysis of capital- ist exploitation and shared the vision of Utopia, but rejected the call to violent revolution. In most countries over the past century the socialist movement was divided between revolutionary and democratic parties, and the struggle between them often took more passion and energy than the battle with capi- talism. But much of the heat went out of the controversy when it became apparent in the 1950s and '60s, even to true believers, that revolutionary communism in the Soviet Union and Eastern Europe was not liberating but oppressive. Communist leaders claimed to be holding power in the interests of the working class during the transition to a socialist society, but they proved to be no exception to Lord Acton's famous dictum, "Power tends to corrupt; absolute power corrupts absolutely." With few checks and balances in the system, the "dictatorship of the proletariat," which was supposed to be democratic, worked no better than other dictatorships.

As Mikhail Gorbachev, perhaps Russia's last Communist ruler, finally dis- covered: "In reorganizing our economic and political system, it is our duty to create, first of all, a dependable and flexible mechanism for the genuine involvement of all the people in deciding state and social matters. Secondly, people must be taught in practice to live in conditions of deepening democra- cy, to extend and consolidate human rights, to nurture a contemporary politi- cal culture; in other words to teach and learn democracy." Thus he attempted to return socialism to its roots, but it was too late for the Communist party – or possibly too early, given the need to work through capitalism before attempting socialism.

Economically, the idea of an economy planned and directed by the state worked well enough in building the industrial foundations of a modern state. Starting with primitive industry, a civil war and economic chaos, the Soviet Union became in less than half a century an economic giant and military superpower. The weaknesses of the system became apparent when growth began to depend more on sophisticated knowledge industries than on steel mills and coal mines, and on the ability to supply a vast range of consumer goods. Centralized planning could not cope as well as markets with all the fac- tors involved in the new economy. As these democratic and economic defects became obvious, there were wholesale defections from Communist parties in the West, and finally in the East.

In sum, there has never been one true socialism, and socialists have always been more interested in goals than means, more critics of capitalism than careful designers of an alternative society. But as socialism emerged as a reac- tion to the horrors of life in the early stages of capitalism, the central idea of all factions was in some way to use the power of the state to liberate the workers from the control of capitalists and thus to create a more equal and fraternal, or co-operative, society, in which individuals would be free to develop to their fullest potential. The ideal behind all the theorizing was bluntly put by George Orwell, best known today for his powerful novels about the horrors of the totalitarian state, *Animal Farm* and *1984.* In his 1930s book on the impoverished life of British miners, *The Road to Wigan Pier,* he concluded with a message to fellow socialists: "The only thing for which we can combine is the underlying ideal of socialism; justice and liberty. But it is hardly strong enough to call this ideal 'underlying.' It is almost completely forgotten. It has been buried beneath layer after layer of doctrinaire priggishness, party squabbles and half-baked 'progressivism' until it is like a diamond hidden under a mountain of dung. The job of the socialist is to get it out again. Justice and liberty!"

One of the most eloquent visions of what a socialist society would be like was offered by Michael Harrington, the U.S. socialist leader and writer whose book *The Other America* revealed the extent of poverty in what was supposed to be an affluent society in the 1960s and encouraged presidents J.F. Kennedy and L.B. Johnson to attempt massive social reform. In a later book, *Socialism* (Saturday Review Press, New York, N.Y., 1972), he wrote:

> This is not an immediate program, constrained by what is politically possible, or even the projection of a middle distance in which structural changes might take place. It is the idea of an utterly new society in which some of the fundamental limitations of human existence have been transcended. Its most basic premise is that man's battle with nature has been completely won and there is therefore more than enough of material goods for everyone. As a result of this unprecedented change in the environment, a psychic mutation takes place: invidious competition is no longer programmed into life by the necessity of a struggle for scarce resources: co-operation, fraternity and equality become natural. In such a world man's social productivity will reach such heights that compulsory work will no longer be necessary. And as more and more things are provided free, money, that universal equivalent by means of which necessities are rationed, will disappear. That, in very brief outline, is what socialism ultimately is. It will never come to pass in its ideal form, yet it is important to detail the dream in order to better design each approximation of it.

THE SYNTHESIS: SOCIAL DEMOCRACY

One version of the Hegelian dialectic, about which more later, is that liberal democracy based on the capitalist economic system has defeated authoritarian Soviet communism and now reigns unchallenged by any other social order. So the dialectic is at an end and history in that sense has ended in the best of all possible social systems. But in my view, while the Soviet Union was a military superpower and the Cold War a major milestone in history, Soviet communism has been an ideological sideshow. The important struggle has been between two visions of democratic society, capitalist and socialist.

In the long struggle of capitalism and socialism, each has had its victories and defeats. For example, the First World War was a shattering defeat for socialists. As war approached, they believed that workers of the world, enlightened by socialism, would refuse to fight in what would be essentially a competition for markets between capitalist countries. In the event, nationalism proved stronger than socialism, and workers in Germany, France, Britain, and other countries, including Canada of course, marched off in their millions to slaughter each other. Russia in particular endured horrendous losses at the front and suffering at home. This revealed the incompetence of the Tsarist autocracy and led to two revolutions: the first established a democratic government of moderate socialists, which in turn was overthrown by revolutionary Communists, called Bolsheviks. The founding of the Union of Soviet Socialist Republics was at first seen by socialists around the world as a victory of vast consequence, but it proved in the long run to be a setback. First, it divided the international socialist movement, as we noted above, and second, its repressive and economically unsuccessful form of government was an easy target for capitalists to point to as a model of "socialism in action."

But despite many setbacks for socialist ideas, it is clear in retrospect that laissez-faire capitalism has been steadily eroded by the power of socialist ideals. There has been incessant pressure on democratic governments to intervene in economic and social affairs to ensure a society kinder and gentler than markets alone can provide. Even anti-socialist politicians have had to respond. For example, concerned by the rise of socialist ideas and parties in Germany in the 1880s, Otto von Bismarck, the "Iron Chancellor," tried first to suppress them, and when that failed, reversed direction and outflanked the socialists by introducing in the 1880s an early model of the welfare state – a tactic known as "anti-socialist socialism."

In Britain, the powerful Liberal party was transformed by the rise of the Labour party on its left and the undeniable need to ease the suffering of workers under capitalism. For example, it changed from being the party of free markets and free trade to being the proponent of government-run schemes of social insurance. The Liberals in Canada followed suit much later, partly because they were threatened by the formation of a socialist party, the Co-operative Commonwealth Federation.

With the Great Depression of the 1930s, capitalism seemed to be collapsing, as socialists had always predicted it would. In Europe, most countries looked rightwards for salvation. Some accepted fascist parties, which preached militant nationalism, denounced international socialism as the enemy, and established state-supervised capitalism. Britain and others clung to traditional conservative parties. But the United States turned left, to Franklin Delano Roosevelt and the New Deal. FDR was no socialist but he did see the need for massive government intervention in a capitalist system in crisis. It has been argued that the economy would have recovered without his efforts but at the minimum he relieved suffering and restored confidence in the social order. (The Conservative government in Canada tried to follow his example, promising "government control and regulation," unemployment and health insurance, and other measures. But it was too late to escape defeat in the 1935 election. In any event, the courts subsequently struck down its proposed New Deal–type legislation on the constitutional grounds that social policy was a provincial and not a federal responsibility.) John Maynard Keynes, another great British economist, published in 1936 his *General Theory of Employment, Interest and Money*, which struck a massive blow at laissez-faire ideas by arguing persuasively that markets would not necessarily end the Depression and restore full employment. While a critic of socialist ideas, he provided theoretical support for government intervention to increase demand when markets were failing to do the job.

But it took the outbreak of the Second World War to force governments to "socialize" their economies in order to mobilize them for military purposes, ending the Depression. In the Allied countries, fear of the outside enemies, Germany and Japan, overcame class and other divisions and made it possible for governments to take actions that would have been unthinkable in peacetime. Labour was conscripted and directed into the armed forces or war work. Wages and prices were controlled, and making excessive profits was condemned as unpatriotic if not downright illegal. National finances were placed under central control. Raw materials were rationed and allocated according to war needs rather than the demands of the market. Artists in all media, from painters to comedians, were enlisted to maintain morale and promote national war aims. Governments encouraged their people to even greater efforts by promising a rosy future in which there would be prosperity and fair shares for all, with homes, jobs, freedom, and opportunity for every citizen. In short, the wartime economies in most democracies were socialistic in practice, although industry remained under private ownership, and the reward for victory was to be a more socialistic society.

In Canada, the opposition party changed its name in 1942 from

Conservative to Progressive Conservative and adopted a program promising sweeping social reform. The Liberal government published in 1943 a *Report on Social Security for Canada,* proposing comprehensive social insurance, family allowances, and health care, and then moved slowly to put in place the foundations of a welfare state. Britain's wartime coalition government, in which Conservatives and Labour party ministers served, began planning social reform long before Victory Day.

Both the politicians and the bureaucrats in the governments of the victorious countries emerged from the war full of confidence in their ability to manage affairs. They had enormous powers to tax, direct, and regulate in their own countries, and they had created international organizations to manage the international markets: principally the International Monetary Fund, which was really a world bank; the World Bank, which was essentially a fund for foreign development; and the General Agreement on Tariffs and Trade. They imposed their goals and methods on the defeated powers, which in any case now saw fascism as a failure and were anxious to emulate their democratic conquerors. Thus, far more than ever before, most of the developed world was socialist in practice and outlook, although it often did not acknowledge or even recognize the ideological source of its policies.

On the other hand, where socialist governments were elected and proceeded to "socialize" major industries – that is, to buy the companies from capitalists and place them under public control as "nationalized" or "Crown" corporations – the new corporations were often unsuccessful. Some socialists would dispute this judgment but the fact remains that over time most socialist governments and parties de-emphasized the notion of public ownership in favour of regulating private ownership to achieve the aims of public policy.

Conservative parties edged left and socialist parties edged right, competing to occupy the centre. Indeed, when the Progressive Conservatives won office in Ottawa in 1957 after some twenty years in opposition, it was only because their new leader, John Diefenbaker, a true prairie populist, had outbid the Liberals by promising better social benefits and more democracy. In Britain, the policies of Labour and Conservative governments were so similar that they were called Butskellism, after R.A. Butler, the leader of the reform wing of the Conservatives, and Hugh Gaitskell, the moderate Labour leader. Republicans won power in the United States by recruiting as their presidential candidate Dwight Eisenhower, a victorious and statesmanlike general who was so middle-of-the-road in politics that he would have been acceptable as Republican or Democrat.

As early as 1959, the West German Social Democratic party, often in the forefront of ideological change in the socialist movement, adopted a new program in which it declared: "Free consumer and job choice as well as free competition and managerial initiative are important elements of Social Democratic economic policy ... A totalitarian economy destroys freedom. Consequently, the Social Democratic party is in favour of free markets whenever true competition exists ... Any concentration of economic power, even in government hands, is dangerous." Only when there was no other way to prevent the concentration of economic power in private hands would public ownership be expedient, and even then it should be decentralized and self-administered. In Canada, the original democratic socialist party, the Co-operative Commonwealth Federation, declared in its founding manifesto in 1933: "No CCF government will rest content until it has eradicated capitalism and put into operation the full program of socialized planning which will lead to the establishment in Canada of the Co-operative Commonwealth." In 1956 this bold statement was replaced with a bromide: "The CCF will not rest content until every person in this land and in all other lands is able to enjoy equality and freedom, a sense of human dignity, and an opportunity to live a rich and meaningful life as a citizen of a free and peaceful world." This, it seemed, was still not enough to reassure Canadian voters, and at the urging of the labour unions, the CCF was transformed in 1961 into the New Democratic Party. While not ruling out public ownership, the new party tacitly accepted that most of the economy would remain in private ownership. When the NDP took power in provinces in Canada, it found that economic reality and public expectations forced it to act much like modern conservative and liberal governments. The story was similar in other Western democracies.

So by now, after more than a century of struggle, we are far removed from laissez-faire capitalism, and also from socialism if that is defined as public ownership of the means of production. Each system of thought has influenced the other, as Hegel would have expected, and we have a synthesis. It is commonly called liberal democracy, or the welfare state, or a mixed economy, or even state capitalism. But these phrases conceal an essential truth: the synthesis is more socialist than capitalist. Democracy in which every citizen has the same basic political rights is established beyond any thought of change, and in fact there is constant pressure and slow progress to extend democratic control. No politician would now dare to deny the goal of equality of opportunity for every citizen, and while this is far from equality of results it does have enormous implications for public policy – for example, equal access to education. In every democracy government manages the economy and is held responsible if it fails to grow and produce wealth, some part of which must be used to advance social justice.

Of course we are still far from the free and equal society of which socialists have always dreamed. There are still huge disparities in wealth, and even in a democracy wealth can buy power. But it is foolish to ignore the progress that has been made toward the goals of the early socialists. And now we can hardly imagine any other way of running our affairs. Thus the common view that capitalism has routed socialism is completely mistaken. The debate between political parties is not about *whether* government should manage the economy and distribute the wealth, but about *how* it can meet those responsibilities.

We have also achieved a form of public ownership of private industry in the sense that pension funds holding the savings of millions of people are huge investors in the private sector of the economy. Trusteed pension funds in Canada hold assets of more than $250 billion, invested on behalf of 3,800,000 working Canadians, a pool of capital second only to that of the chartered banks. In the United States it is estimated that the funds own about half the stocks and bonds of the major corporations. In both countries the share of investment capital held by pension funds is constantly growing. But as the funds are professionally managed, the investors have no control over the corporations, and it is therefore a mistake to view this situation as "pension fund socialism," as it has been called.

The best term for this synthesis is social democracy. But, again, this is a tricky phrase which has changed its meaning in the past and probably will again. In the early days of the socialist movement, revolutionaries were termed social democrats, partly because democracy itself was a revolutionary idea. Now, people who call themselves social democrats are often former socialists who have come to accept that private ownership and enterprise in a market economy work better than state ownership. But in practice most major parties in the democracies, including liberals and conservatives, are now social democratic. Of course, they would never admit as much because the more alike the parties are in reality, the more they have to pretend they are different, in the manner of giant corporations which market almost identical products but spend millions on advertising to persuade consumers they are different.

The truth is that the Great Depression was proof enough for most that laissez-faire capitalism is not acceptable in a democratic society. It may be the most efficient way to generate economic growth but that growth is not, as the popular metaphor suggests, "a rising tide [that] lifts all boats." The rising tide in a harbour does indeed lift all boats, from liners to skiffs, and at the same rate. But the tide of capitalist growth lifts people at very different rates, making some undeservedly rich and leaving others unjustly poor. Further, tides that rise also fall, and the cycle of boom and bust is too socially disruptive to be tolerated in a democracy in which majority opinion rules.

In the postwar social democratic period in the Western democracies, almost continuous economic growth provided millions of high-wage jobs for industrial workers. Government programs ensured there would be affordable housing, income support in hard times, health care, and education for everyone's children. In Canada, after allowing for inflation, average incomes rose 34 percent in the decade of the 1940s, 43 percent in the '50s, and 37 percent in the '60s. Working-class families in all the democracies began to think of themselves as middle class, with a boundless future, provided governments managed things sensibly. In short, there was a "revolution in expectations," which eroded class distinctions, ideologies, and party loyalties, seeming to prove that Marx had been fundamentally wrong when he insisted that capitalism would inevitably impoverish the masses. The synthesis of social democracy became the new thesis, the conventional wisdom of the day supported by all right-thinking people. The different programs offered by political parties, and fiercely debated by partisans of left and right, were all in fact within the broad framework of social democracy.

This is the cause of much of the public frustration today with parties, politicians, and the political process. The system does not work nearly as well as it once did (for reasons to be discussed in the next chapter) but no obvious alternative is available. Debate between the parties is sterile, and new leaders and new governments turn out to be just as ineffective as the old ones because they all work within the same outdated framework of acceptable means and desirable ends.

CHAPTER TWO

THE CRISIS OF SOCIAL DEMOCRACY

In a social democracy, as we have seen, the means of production are mostly privately owned and the economy is driven by competition in the market, but the government is responsible for ensuring the system works smoothly and for distributing the national income. This has meant in practice that the government operates the levers of economic policy – spending, taxation, the money supply, regulation of markets to encourage fair competition, and, occasionally, wage and price controls – to try to ensure a level of demand that will encourage steady growth without inflation. National income is distributed according to priorities roughly set by the public in elections. By choosing one party rather than another, the public decides in the broadest way what priorities to accord to incomes, profits, public investment, and social spending ranging from health care to regional economic development. The actual business of generating the national income by producing and selling goods and services at home and abroad is left to private enterprise.

To describe the system is not to say that it has always worked as intended. The public sometimes demands more than the economy can deliver and politicians rashly promise to provide it. Governments make bad decisions because they are competing with opposition parties for public favour, or simply because they misread the economic signals. In the private sector of a comfortable social democracy, business decision-makers may be less enterprising than foreign competitors, overburdened with taxation and regulation, or unable to cope with demanding workers in strong labour unions. We have suffered all these failures and more, but in its heyday (roughly 1945–70) social democracy certainly worked better than the boom-and-bust capitalism of the past. Governments were reasonably successful in managing growth and distributing the income in a way that kept all groups satisfied. And the whole process was consistent with the ideals of democracy – something which cannot be said of capitalism. People who have achieved political sovereignty, that is to say, the right to vote and choose a government, will not want to entrust their economic sovereignty to markets over which they have no control. Nor will they allow the proceeds of growth to be distributed without regard for the priorities of the majority.

Things started to go wrong with social democracy in the 1960s, but it was thought to be merely a problem of fine-tuning a successful system. By the 1970s it was clear that the problems were more fundamental. Economies slowed or even stagnated while at the same time prices rose, something that wasn't supposed to happen in a well-managed economy. The inflation eroded wage increases so much that the average real improvement in Canada was only 8.5 percent in the '70s and a miserable 2 percent in the '80s, and unemployment soared. The phenomenon of stagnant economies with rising prices was termed "stagflation," and millions, probably billions, of words have been written by economists and others to try to explain what went wrong and why. Was it the energy crisis caused by the cartel of oil-producing countries driving up the price of the fuel on which the industrial world depended? Was it the legacy of President Lyndon Johnson, who tried to pay for the Vietnam war without raising taxes? Or was it, as monetarists claimed, simply that governments had expanded the money supply so recklessly, so far beyond real growth in the economy, that each dollar was worth less and prices had to rise? Even if it is correct, this theory does not explain why governments were so imprudent in the first place. The answer to that may be the revolution in expectations. To win the votes of people who had grown to believe that everything was possible, politicians bid against each other and then tried to finance their promises by increasing the money supply. If that is indeed what happened, it was not a fatal flaw in social democracy, as some conservatives began to say, but a mistake to be corrected – a lesson to be learnt by people seeking for the first time to control their economic fate. The important fact for our analysis is that neither governments nor opposition parties knew how to deal with this setback for social democracy.

Most governments tried to check inflation with some form of income and price controls, a form of economic planning. Ironically, the strongest opposition came from labour unions, which claimed to favour economic planning but demanded in practice the right to sell labour for the highest wages they could obtain in a free market. When controls proved impracticable in the long term, governments and their central bankers reverted to a more primitive but effective method. They squeezed the supply of money so that interest rates rose, business activity slowed, profits fell, unemployment climbed, and workers could no longer bargain for higher wages. In short, they induced a recession. In addition, although few realized it at the time, the long postwar boom was coming to an end, and a contradiction had appeared in the thesis of social democracy.

The first impulse is to say that the antithesis was provided by Prime

Minister Margaret Thatcher in Britain and President Ronald Reagan in the United States. They were upstarts in their own conservative parties who argued that the problem was not some technical difficulty with the machinery of social democracy (or socialism as they preferred to call it) but the whole idea of social democracy. Government, they said, had become so big and taxes had risen so high that they were stifling markets and enterprise. Their solution was to "roll back socialism" by cutting taxes to encourage capitalistic enterprise, selling off to private owners publicly owned corporations, deregulating privately owned industries, and cutting or at least capping social services. In other words, these neo-conservatives, as they were mistakenly called, were not advancing new ideas but seeking to return to an earlier form of capitalism – an earlier stage in the dialectic between capitalism and socialism. But despite their rhetoric they did not in fact propose to roll back far because neither dared to renounce the central pillar of social democracy, which is that governments, not markets, are ultimately responsible for national economic performance and social welfare. They did not propose to return to laissez-faire capitalism. And while the voters applauded their attacks on bloated bureaucracies and wasteful programs, they also continued to demand new and better government services, so that the Thatcher and Reagan regimes could not significantly reduce the size of government.

It's arguable, in fact, that government intervention in the U.S. economy increased during the Reagan years as budget deficits rose at an unprecedented rate. In any event, the Reagan/Thatcher measures produced only short-lived booms, followed by public revulsion at the greed that drove the erratic markets and the callous disregard on the part of those who profited for those who fell behind. Even Reagan's vice-president and successor, George Bush, recognized the need for a kinder and gentler society. Thatcher's policies divided British society so bitterly that her own party dumped her. In Canada, the role of government was so firmly entrenched – for reasons to be discussed in the next chapter – that Prime Minister Brian Mulroney's Conservative governments never seriously attempted to follow the Thatcher-Reagan ideology, although of course they were accused of doing so. Thus the Thatcher-Reagan ideas were not a new antithesis but probably the last gasp of the old dialectic. Their failure merely reconfirmed the thesis of social democracy – despite its weaknesses, which became ever more obvious as economies plunged into the worst recession in half a century.

The real problem with social democracy as we have known and loved it is that it was designed to work within national economies whereas most of us now live in economies that are continental in some respects and global in others. National governments have lost much of their power of economic management, and thus the ability to ensure growth and use the proceeds to raise the level of social justice. To take one simple example, governments used to respond to a downturn in the private business cycle by increasing public spending in order to put more money into the pockets of consumers. As long as the money was spent mainly on goods and services produced within the country, this worked well enough to stimulate demand, production, and employment. Now that many if not most of the things we buy are produced in other countries, an increase in consumption at home goes partly to stimulate foreign economies. And because many of the goods and services we produce are exported for sale in other countries, our levels of growth, income, and employment depend on the levels of demand abroad – beyond the control of our governments.

It is a similar story with the other main tool of economic management, the money supply. Once our governments could raise or lower the supply according to what they deemed to be our national interest, slowing or accelerating our economy without much regard for what other countries were doing. But now capital moves across national borders even more easily than goods and services, flowing at the touch of a computer key to where it can earn the highest return. If we get far out of step with our competitors, either capital will flee or more than we need will flow in, which can also disrupt our economy. Less directly but with equally serious impact on national economic sovereignty, cross-border mass media – principally TV and films – establish international norms of the good life to which we think we are entitled. If all Americans are represented as having colour televisions, home computers, and holidays in Florida, so should we enjoy the same luxuries, even if our economy does not earn enough to provide them, and woe betide the politician who says that the correct policy for us is to reduce personal consumption and increase investment.

The debt and deficit problems from which we now suffer are partly the result of governments trying to deal with new economic problems by old-fashioned methods. Faced with slow or zero growth, or with recession, and with unemployment rising, they assumed the problem was inadequate demand. To deal with this they borrowed and spent heavily to put money in consumers' pockets and increase demand. In reality, much of the problem was the result of worldwide economic change beyond the control of any nation, even the mighty United States. No matter how much we borrowed and spent, we could not escape change at home when international circumstances were changing and dragging us along with them. All we did was to pile up a huge national debt and slow down the inevitable restructuring of our own economy.

Governments and most political parties are now adjusting to the new realities, but many Canadians (in fact probably the vast majority) have yet to accept fully that the economic sovereignty of all nations is now severely restricted. Some people simply deny the obvious because they find it uncomfortable, and they are encouraged by opportunistic politicians, ideologues, and labour leaders who promise to return us to an earlier and less competitive era in which national social democracy worked very well. There is no way back, and while there is no reliable vision of the future, a great deal depends on how well we adjust to inescapable change.

From earliest times business has crossed borders in search of higher profits, usually by way of two-way trade and sometimes with the help of governments that used armed force to conquer new markets. New technologies encouraged the process. For example, when steamships replaced sailing vessels, trade became faster and safer; railways made huge markets possible in countries spanning whole continents; and the telegraph speeded the exchange of business information and credit. But in this half-century an explosion of new technologies has made possible – and therefore inevitable – explosive acceleration in the process of internationalizing business. Computers and satellites make communication almost instantaneous, and jet aircraft speed the passage of people and goods. National borders have become increasingly irrelevant, and the Industrial Revolution has been spread to hitherto remote and underdeveloped parts of the world.

Canada was in a sense a pioneer in the process of internationalizing business. We were developed first by British and then by American capital. In what was probably a misguided attempt to foster our own industrialization in the last century, we raised tariffs against U.S. manufactures. The result was that U.S. corporations hopped the border and set up subsidiaries here to serve the small Canadian market. This current became a tidal wave after the Second World War, when U.S. business was expanding all over the non-Communist world. In the medium term this was good for economic growth and employment in Canada. But there were serious limiting factors: these subsidiary companies imported technology and often managers from the United States; their costs were high because our market was small and spread thin; and they were not interested in export trade, which would have meant competing with their parent corporations. So we developed an inefficient industrial base which was bound to suffer severely when exposed to global competition.

Economic nationalists argue that had we raised our tariff barriers even higher against U.S. goods and services, borrowed U.S. capital instead of accepting it as investment in subsidiaries, and rented U.S. technology, we could have built strong Canadian-owned manufacturing companies. That might have been possible, but only in the very unlikely event that Canadians had been willing to accept slower growth and a lower standard of living than in the neighbour to the south. But in any case, giant U.S. manufacturing companies have now been undermined, even bankrupted, by foreign competition and there is no reason to suppose that Canadian enterprises would have done better. The fact is that mass production manufacturing is shifting to other parts of the world, and both the U.S. and Canada are being forced to seek new ways of earning their living in competitive global markets.

After the Second World War the United States and to a lesser extent Canada aided both allies and former enemies to rebuild their shattered economies. And as former colonies became independent, we undertook to help them develop their economies, with aid and trade, never imagining for a moment that they might one day become fierce competitors. Remembering that national economic protectionism had precipitated or at least worsened the Great Depression of the 1930s, most countries signed the General Agreement on Tariffs and Trade, which provided for gradual reduction in barriers to trade – that is to say, progress toward freer world trade. All this plus new technologies was bound to bring about fundamental economic change, and we had plenty of warning of what was coming.

In 1973 the U.S. sociologist Daniel Bell documented the shift in the U.S. economy from manufacturing to services in his seminal book on *The Coming of Post-Industrial Society* (Basic Books, New York). In the same year the United Nations counted thousands of corporations which were international in the sense that they were operating in more than one country. More than two hundred were truly multinational (MNCs), each having subsidiaries in more than twenty countries, between which they transferred capital, technology, goods, and services, paying as little attention as they could to national boundaries. Reports of two government commissions set up in Canada – the 1968 Watkins report and the 1972 Gray report – had already acknowledged, if somewhat reluctantly, that MNCs were here to stay, and that they brought to Canada capital, technology, and access to export markets. Against these advantages was the fact that they encroached on Canadian economic sovereignty. The problem was how to maximize the advantages and minimize the disadvantages or, in other words, how to square the circle.

The Economic Council of Canada, in a far-sighted 1975 report (titled *Looking Outward*), discussed global economic trends and the impact they would have on Canada. The report pointed to the emergence of three economic superpowers, the United States, Japan, and the European Community, each with its own trading bloc. It also noted that new, efficient, and low-cost manufacturers were appearing in Asia and elsewhere. "Business enterprises in the future," the authors continued, "will be increasingly research oriented and the most advanced countries will tend to develop and export technological know-how, follow-up services, and a variety of other intangible products in which the principal ingredient is intellectual capital." The council recommended that Canada prepare for the new economy by opening itself to free trade, if possible with all three economic superpowers, but if necessary with the United States alone. Competition would then force hitherto protected and truncated Canadian corporations to move from standard manufacturing to new industries based on research, high technical skills, and sophisticated management. But rather than face up to new economic challenges Canadians and their governments spent much of the 1960s and '70s trying to avoid them.

They feared that for this country internationalization would mean increasing U.S. influence and eventually loss of the national identity. So instead of welcoming the stimulus of free trade they retreated into forms of protectionism. And although economic blocs were emerging in Europe and Asia, they tried in various ways to loosen their economic ties with the United States. In 1972 the Trudeau government adopted the so-called "Third Option," sponsored by External Affairs Minister Mitchell Sharp, which caused some excitement. The option argued that "Canada can pursue a comprehensive, long-term strategy to develop and strengthen the Canadian economy and other aspects of its national life and in the process to reduce the present Canadian vulnerability." The strategy was to include policies to alter the industrial structure of Canada, but as Sharp recently conceded, "This was never really seriously attempted and, in retrospect, was probably far too difficult an undertaking for any federal government of Canada, given the crucial role of the provinces with respect both to resources and industry" (*Which Reminds Me ... A Memoir,* University of Toronto Press, 1994).

This was the obvious weakness in all the talk about national industrial strategies by which the federal government would make the economy more competitive by picking and supporting "winning" industries. In fact, the one major strategy attempted, the 1980 National Energy Program, produced a crisis in national unity. World oil prices were soaring and this promised a bonanza for the oil-producing provinces, particularly Alberta. When Ottawa attempted to limit prices within Canada for the benefit of other provinces and to siphon off some of the profits to finance national economic development, the West exploded with rage, and the wounds have not yet fully healed. As it turned out, the premise of continually rising prices on which the federal strategy had been based proved to be wrong anyway.

All the economic nationalists' efforts were in vain and a dangerous waste of time and energy. We could no more turn back the tide of North American economic integration – a stage in the larger process of economic globalization – than King Canute could halt the rising tide that lapped his throne on the seashore. Despite twenty years of the best efforts of Canadian governments, the share of Canadian trade going to the United States increased, and capital flowed both ways across the border as Canadian and U.S. corporations sought

continental markets. The real choice was not between nationalism and conti-
nentalism; it was whether to leave continental integration entirely to market
forces or to regulate it in some degree by a Canada-U.S. treaty, which would
phase in the reduction of barriers and establish a binational mechanism for
resolving disputes.

By the 1980s, the Liberal government was having second thoughts about
trade policy. Prime Minister Trudeau promoted trilateral U.S.-Mexico-
Canada meetings to seek what he called "commonality of views," and in 1982
he appointed the Royal Commission on Economic Union and Development
Prospects for Canada, chaired by a senior Liberal, Donald S. Macdonald, to
explore all the options. In 1983, the government published a discussion paper
on trade policy suggesting free trade with the United States in selected economic sectors. By the time the Macdonald commission reported in 1985, the
Conservatives were in power, but its recommendation of free trade gave the
new government a hefty shove. It was thus Liberals, and not the Mulroney
Conservatives as generally thought, who put free trade on the Canadian agenda, although it was left to the Conservatives to negotiate first a deal with the
U.S. and then an extension to Mexico (NAFTA). In opposition, the Liberals
were fierce critics of Conservative trade policies, promising at one stage to
"tear up" the Canada-U.S. Free Trade Agreement. But this was merely party
politics, and if one listened carefully, what the Liberals were really saying was
that they were not opposed to free trade, but only to the deals the Conservatives had negotiated. In office again, they ratified NAFTA with only cos-
metic changes. Free trade was supported also by the two new regional parties,
the Bloc Québécois and the western-based Reform party. Thus continental
free trade became a broadly accepted national policy. It had taken governments about twenty years to come to grips with reality.

Of course there are still many Canadians opposed to free trade, and it is
not by chance that they are principally represented in politics by the two organizations that claim to be the leading voices of social democracy, the New
Democratic Party and the Canadian Labour Congress. They believe, correctly,
that free trade encroaches upon national sovereignty, making it hard if not
impossible for government in Canada to manage the economy because multinational corporations can shift investment and employment to countries that
offer them the most profitable environment. In fact, anything that encourages
economic internationalization, including the free movement of capital, undermines social democracy as long as it is based on national sovereignty.

But what social democrats in Canada refuse to accept is that the age of
national economic sovereignty has passed, and with it the ability of national
governments to manage their economies. When they insist that by cancelling
the free-trade deals we could restore sovereignty, prosperity, and the heyday of

social democracy, they are being reactionary rather than progressive. To opt out of continentalization and globalization would in the short term protect us from foreign competition, but it is competition that guarantees efficiency, and it is efficiency that produces growth. Interestingly, the British Labour party, which was the model for democratic socialism in Canada, fiercely opposed entry into the European Common Market until it came to see that integration with Europe was necessary to ensure economic growth, and that growth was necessary to preserve social democracy. Now Labour works to introduce into Britain the European Social Charter while the Conservative government worries about national sovereignty. If the NDP wishes to regain the political ground it has lost, it will have to accept the new economic realities, as the Labour party has done in Britain.

But what precisely are those realities? Many futurists argue that as we approach the twenty-first century we are entering an era in which new technologies – computers, gene-splicing, and so on – will bring about changes as profound as those produced in the nineteenth century by the Industrial Revolution. But our problems are here now, and – let's be frank about this – we cannot predict what is going to happen in even the next few years. In fact, we can't even make a good guess. The stores are stacked with books that make confident predictions, often contradicting each other. Some bestsellers insist that the world is plunging into a depression that will make the 1930s look like the good old days; others see a vast new boom just over the horizon. In the newspapers and financial journals some "experts" see stock markets going up and others are sure they are already overpriced and due to crash. Are we sinking into deflation, or is it inflation that is going to be the problem? Are interest rates, the price of gold, employment, the value of the Canadian dollar going up or down? Is the world moving toward freer trade for all, or to the development of regional trading blocs, or to a return of protectionism? Or perhaps toward some of each of the above, with the European Community, the North American countries, and Asia led by the Japanese (or Chinese) each encouraging free trade within the bloc and protection against outsiders? The United States is today the strongest economy, but is it now, like all other empires before it, overextended and beginning an irreversible decline, or are its best days still to come? Pick the economic question and you can find a dozen different and contradictory answers, at least half of which must be proved wrong by events.

But those who believe we can return to the age of national sovereignty are certainly wrong. Technology has made global integration possible and market forces will ensure it happens because it is more economically efficient. Where once national states grew much of their own food, mined and pumped their own raw materials, manufactured their own goods, and produced their own services, from fast-food restaurants to the most advanced science, they are now being forced by competition to concentrate on what they do best – to exploit the advantages they have in comparison with other countries.

The comparative advantage – as economists put it – of developing countries is unskilled labour ready to work long days for low wages in grimy factories because it is preferable to subsistence farming. These countries are experiencing the industrial revolution that transformed Europe and the United States in the nineteenth century. Describing the rapid industrialization of China, the American writer Paul Theroux said, "The dynamo of capitalism has been loosed ... It is a sight the likes of which few people alive today have seen ... The cities of south China are functioning versions of towns that are familiar to anyone who has lived in an urban area in Europe or America where the factories are now empty and the machines have stopped" (*Harper's*, October 1993). One key to their success is that workers enjoy only limited democracy and civil rights and are disciplined by a conformist culture in which government and business are committed to capitalist-led development. In other words, these countries emphasize the economic values of Western social democracy but de-emphasize the political values. Asian countries in particular claim that this form of capitalism is a unique product of their culture, but in fact it is not much different from the situation in Europe during the early days of the Industrial Revolution, before socialist and trade-union organizers raised the expectations of the working class.

The obvious comparative advantage of the developed countries is that they have the capital, technology, and consumer markets that the newly industrialized countries need to build and operate their factories, and to keep them busy. Many European, North American, and Japanese corporations that used to manufacture and market within one country now operate multinationally to bring together the comparative advantages of several countries – development capital from one, technology from another, cheap labour from a third, and consumer markets around the world. This is not the pattern with all manufacturing, nor is it to say that all manufacturing will eventually move to low-wage areas. But the manufacturing that remains in developed companies will be automated to keep employment and labour costs low, and jobs in manufacturing industries will tend to be for researchers, managers, and skilled technicians.

Developed countries like Canada have the educational, research, and technological base from which to generate new knowledge, new and better ways of doing things, and entirely new products and services now only dimly perceived or yet undreamed of. As Peter F. Drucker, the dean of American business theorists, has argued:

The basic economic resource – the "means of production" to use the economist's term – is no longer capital, nor natural resources (the economist's "land"), nor "labour." *It is and will be knowledge.* The central wealth-creating activities will be neither the allocation of capital to productive uses, nor "labour" – the two poles of nineteenth and twentieth-century economic theory, whether classical, Marxist, Keynesian, or neo-classical. Value is now created by "productivity" and "innovation," both applications of knowledge to work. (*Post-Capitalist Society,* Harper Collins, New York, 1993)

The knowledge society, he said, is post-capitalist, because knowledge workers own both the means of production through their pension funds and the tools of production in the knowledge they carry with them.

This vision is cold comfort for millions of workers who have seen the unskilled or semi-skilled mass-production jobs, which once earned them middle-class incomes, departing to Asia or Latin America or even to post-Communist Eastern Europe. Nor is it much help to the clerks and middle managers who lose their jobs as corporations automate – that is to say, as corporations cut costs and raise productivity by applying new knowledge to work that used to be theirs. Speaking at a conference on NAFTA in 1992, when he was minister-counsellor at the U.S. Embassy in Ottawa, Larry Taylor reflected on this problem:

Two hundred years ago the Luddites threw their wooden tools into the machines of the Industrial Revolution, and it's a word that has come to describe people who are reactionary and backward. That may be wrong; it's more complicated. The industrial revolution laid the groundwork for the prosperity the world knows today. It also displaced those people, cost them their jobs, their way of livelihood. It's no wonder they threw their wooden tools into those machines; those machines would destroy what they thought was important in life ... In this technology-driven world it's possible that the automobile and smokestack industries that employ a lot of people are history. Information processing, the knowledge industries, bio-genetics, bio-technology are the economic history of the future, and it's exploding. It's just possible we are living through another time like that [the Industrial Revolution] and people are concerned. The Luddites couldn't be convinced that it was good for them, and they shouldn't have been; it wasn't good for them, it was good for society in the long run. I think you do have to pay attention to the real problems [caused by] this rapid, technology-driven restructuring the world is going through – environmental problems, social problems – and it's only when people are convinced those fears are being adequately heard and taken care of that they can come to support the kinds of change that are inherent in such rapid technological shifts.

Undoubtedly Taylor was right in advocating, in effect, more social democracy – social solutions to problems caused by economic change. However, both the economic change and the social problems are international in origin and subject in only a limited degree to national solutions. And solutions that inhibit economic change by raising costs faster than productivity, or by retarding restructuring, will in the end make the problems worse. The great social democracies, which is to say the developed countries, are experimenting in a dozen different forums on ways to co-ordinate national policies in the common interest of ensuring that competition is fair and not cutthroat. Trade treaties now extend to cover such related subjects as the environment, labour adjustment, and to some extent civil rights. The UN, after years of stagnation, is beginning to write and try to enforce new rules for national behaviour, and is proposing a world social charter to end extremes of poverty.

We are accepting, slowly and reluctantly, the fact that economic globalization is making national states increasingly irrelevant. Those who persist in arguing that we can return to the comfortable days of social democracy within sovereign national states merely make the process more difficult. But what we require is a new vision of social democracy to replace the old. It must be global in ambition, embracing "workers of the world" in practice as well as in rhetoric, with the goal of social justice for all. This probably means that at least in the short and middle terms it should be a social democratic version of supply-side economics, in which the focus is on generating growth rather than distributing wealth. In the global context, growth should be in the newly industrializing countries, while incomes in the developed countries rise much more slowly than has been our experience, stabilize, or even fall. Social democrats have always believed in redistributing wealth from rich to poor within national societies; in the global society we in the developed world are the rich.

The priorities of governments should be to help people adjust to the economic change that is being forced on them by markets, and to spread the burdens of adjustment fairly. That will involve education and training of the work force, and research and development; it also means building social consensus for measures such as sharing jobs and accepting lower incomes for less work. But it is much easier to describe ends than to devise means of getting there, and globalization demands a wrenching change of consciousness for minds focused on national states and policies. This will be more difficult in Canada than in many other countries, for reasons to be explored in the next chapter.

While we struggle to adjust, we have to survive in a global economy in which, in the final analysis, every worker is in competition with every other worker in the world. Marshall McLuhan coined the term "global village" to describe a world drawn together by the instant communication of electric media. It has become a cliché, and like many clichés it is misleading. The village in normal usage is a small, friendly, and stable community made up of good neighbours living similar lives. But while the globe has shrunk and there is a sense of interdependence among nations, it is less a village than a vast metropolis in which there are the homes of the rich and the slums of the poor, areas lined with squalid factories and others with the gleaming skyscrapers. The streets are shared by affluent shoppers, hurrying workers, and unemployed beggars. Urban violence is endemic. Canada is in the high-rent district of this metropolis, but we can continue to earn the rent only by exploiting our comparative advantages. Resisting change or trying to redistribute income we don't have will move us swiftly into the slums – and Canadians who want a better life will have to move to another part of town: that is, emigrate, perhaps to China to work on the electronic highway.

CHAPTER THREE

THE CANADIAN SICKNESS

The crisis of social democracy based on national states is a problem throughout the Western world where, as we have seen, it has become the ruling ideology. But it is particularly serious in Canada because our national identity is founded on social democracy. We believe that our commitment to social democracy is what distinguishes us from the United States and justifies our separate existence. Because they rebelled against British rule and rejected British institutions, Americans had to invent their own political culture. This they did with the Declaration of Independence, their constitution, which replaced the original Articles of Confederation, and the amendments known as the Bill of Rights. These were acts of extraordinarily creative statesmanship, setting out the basic values of the nation and designing a unique system of government to put them into practice. Having been sanctified in a civil war, they have become symbols to which all Americans give allegiance without question, and the country is governed by the rules they established. In contrast, the Fathers of the Canadian Confederation saw no need to debate and define a political culture. They were loyal subjects of Britain at the height of its Victorian glory, and indeed Canada existed in large part because its peoples had refused to join the American Revolution.

The speeches during the debates on Confederation in the legislature of what was then the Province of Canada (Ontario and Quebec) reveal the reservations some of the leaders had about U.S. popular democracy and about federalism, which seemed to have led the United States into a ruinous civil war. As Donald Creighton, the great conservative historian, put it in *Canada's First Century* (Macmillan of Canada, 1970):

> They were typical mid-Victorian colonial politicians who were intellectually as remote from the eighteenth-century preoccupation with political first principles as they were from the twentieth-century obsession with ethnic and cultural values. They thought of themselves as British subjects, and assumed that they were the legitimate heirs of the British constitutional heritage and full participants in the British political experience. Alone among all the colonies that European

nations had founded in the New World, the British American colonies had never sought to separate themselves from the Motherland ... Constitutional monarchy, parliamentary institutions, and responsible government made up a political tradition which was not only British but also British American. The Fathers of Confederation assumed, without question, that this political tradition must be continued unimpaired in the nation they were creating.

The French-Canadian Fathers were presumably less influenced by the British example than their English-speaking colleagues, but they were conservative in their attachment to their language, their culture, and the Catholic Church. Quebec had not participated in the French Revolution, and its society was descended from the old France. There was no attraction for them in being swallowed up in the English-speaking and revolutionary United States. A Canadian confederation in which they would enjoy a measure of sovereignty was the best course available (and remained so until independence became a reasonable possibility about a century later). So rather than invent a new political culture for a vast new country, different in almost every imaginable way from Britain, the Fathers declared, in the British North America Act creating Confederation, that Canada would have a constitution "similar in principle to that of the United Kingdom."

This was at best misleading, because the BNA Act went on to specify a federal system unlike Britain's unitary system, the first of many contradictions and confusions that have made it so hard for Canadians to understand, let alone love, their political culture. We'll look more closely later at the problems of Confederation. But if the Canadian constitution was ambiguous – or, worse, a political deception – the British model of government, which the Canadians so unthinkingly adopted, also had large elements of smoke and mirrors. It is sufficient here to note that the parliamentary system evolved from centuries of ideological and class struggle. Even the benches for the opposing party leaders are set two sword-lengths apart so that they cannot lunge at each other. The historic achievements of the British House of Commons were to wrest power first from the autocratic crown and then from the lords, and to establish a form of government by consent of the middle class. With the Industrial Revolution and the organization in the last century of mass parties to represent different classes, the Commons became a forum for a civilized form of class struggle. The Conservatives by and large represented the well-to-do, and the Labour party the less well-off, until they converged on social democracy.

But in Canada regional and cultural differences have always been more important than ideologies based on class, and these can be resolved only by conciliation and compromise. The regions need to see that their points of view are expressed in the national legislature and taken into account by government, that their interests, languages, and customs are represented and respected when national policies are made. If there has to be a compromise, they have to understand what they are getting and giving, and why. This is almost never the case in a House of Commons with an all-powerful, one-party government on one side and a powerless opposition on the other.

POLITICAL CULTURE AND IDEOLOGIES

We have been slow to change a system that clearly does not work, and one reason is that we adopted, with British political institutions, a conservative political culture. But what is meant in this context by conservative, and what does it have to do with social democracy? Even at the expense of digressing from the line of argument it is necessary to define terms that have become confused in their passage from Europe to North America. The popular way of thinking about the spectrum of political beliefs is along a horizontal line from socialism on the left through liberalism in the centre to conservatism on the right, but this is profoundly misleading. In reality, the socialists and conservatives have more in common than either has with liberals. Rather than a straight line, therefore, think of a horseshoe with socialists and conservatives separate but quite near each other at the ends, and liberals away in the centre.

Liberals, in the traditional sense of that term, view society as a collection of individuals, each of whom is entitled to pursue his or her own idea of happiness with the minimum of interference by the state. This implies limited government, the rule of law to protect the rights of the individual, including the right to own property, a free market for goods and ideas, and a society tolerant of all sorts of beliefs and lifestyles. True conservatism views society not as a collection of individuals, but as an organic community in which there is a natural hierarchy of authority, and individuals have both rights and duties. Conservatives believe that there is in every person an element of original sin, and they are sceptical therefore about the possibility of perfecting human society. All this implies the need for strong government to keep order, in alliance with strong churches to prescribe moral values. Nevertheless, it is the task of government to protect the public interest against excesses of private power, and to improve society – but slowly and carefully. However, government may itself become a tyranny, and so there is a need for other, private centres of power – barons to curb the king in times past, now the business class and even labour unions and media to balance the state. For conservatives, the savage in all of us is always at the gate, civilization is hard won, and things are just as likely to get worse as they are to get better. Therefore, they are sceptical about the notion that change is progress, they honour tradition and seek above all a stable and orderly society.

Socialists also see society as a community and believe in strong government to advance the common interest. But they are more optimistic than conservatives and believe in the essential goodness of men and women. It is only the imperfections of the system that prevent the perfection of the individual. Those imperfections are the rotten fruit of history: the tyranny of the ruling class, the exploitation of the poor by the rich in an unequal marketplace in which labour is just another commodity, the corruption of values by repressive religions. Democracy offers the masses the opportunity to change all this by winning and expanding the power of the state, thereby mastering the power of private capital, abolishing privilege, and promoting fraternity and equality.

Modern party labels clearly do not match these traditional definitions, and this has caused a great deal of confusion among politicians as well as the news media and the public. Thus Margaret Thatcher called herself a conservative but was really a radical liberal. Ronald Reagan was said in the U.S. to be a neo-conservative but was really a liberal. In Canada, the Conservative party has flirted recently with classical liberalism, but its true roots are in traditional conservatism, sometimes called toryism, so much so in fact that some members were known as Red Tories. Gad Horowitz, who coined this happy term, defined it in a well-known essay in which he pointed to the similarities between toryism and socialism:

> Since tory and socialist minds have some critical assumptions and values in common, there is a positive affinity between them. From certain angles they appear not as enemies, but as two different expressions of the same outlook. This helps to explain the Canadian phenomenon of the *red* tory. At the simplest level, he is a tory who prefers the socialists to the liberals, or a socialist who prefers the tories to the liberals, without really knowing why. At a higher level, he is a conscious ideological tory with some "odd" socialist notions ... or a conscious ideological socialist with some "odd" tory notions ... At the very highest level, he is a philosopher who combines elements of socialism and of toryism so thoroughly in a single integrated Weltanschauung that it is impossible to say he is a proponent of either one or the other. (*Canada: A Guide to the Peaceable Kingdom,* ed. William Kilbourn, Macmillan of Canada, 1970)

The Liberal party, as we have seen, long ago abandoned classical liberalism, and the socialists now generally recognize themselves as social democrats. Here endeth the digression into definitions, and we return to Canadian political culture.

THE DECLINE OF CONSERVATISM

Conservatism was the governing ideology at Confederation, with ideas and values that were supposed to set us apart from U.S. liberalism. The conservatism of the time, wrote George Grant, the philosopher and political polemicist, "was an inchoate desire to build, in these cold and forbidding regions, a society with a greater sense of order and restraint than freedom-loving republicanism would allow. It was no better defined than a kind of suspicion that we in Canada could be less lawless and have a greater sense of propriety than the United States ... [It] was essentially the social doctrine that public order and tradition, in contrast to freedom and experiment, were central to the good life" (*Lament for a Nation: The Defeat of Canadian Nationalism,* McClelland and Stewart, 1965). This emphasis on order is central to conservatism, and Pierre Berton has pointed out perceptively (in his book *Why We Act Like Canadians,* McClelland and Stewart, 1982) that its icon in Canada is the Mountie. On the U.S. frontier sheriffs elected by the community enforced the law. In Canada, it was a member of a paramilitary force representing the Crown.

Not all the Fathers were politically conservative, but John A. Macdonald was, and it was he who led and shaped the young country in its first years. So also were the institutions: the Crown at the pinnacle of a hierarchy of authority centralized in Ottawa; the vast powers of the cabinet when supported by a majority in the House of Commons (as opposed to the checks and balances of the U.S. constitution); the appointed Senate to protect the rights of property against the excesses of the democratic Commons; the guarantees for Roman Catholic and Protestant schools. The way in which these values distinguished Canada from the United States was neatly summarized by W.L. Morton, a distinguished Canadian scholar, in a collection of lectures published under the title *The Canadian Identity* (University of Wisconsin Press, 1961). The difference, he said, was the difference between "Life, Liberty and the pursuit of Happiness" promised in the liberal U.S. Declaration of Independence, and "peace, order and good government" promised in the conservative British North America Act. He explained:

> Canadians, if one may judge by their history, believe that society cannot live by the state alone. Society has its own autonomous life, which is sustained by sources which may enrich the life of the state, but over which the state has neither authority nor control. Those sources are religious or moral and flow into society only through persons. The personality of the individual citizen, then, is the object of the justice the state exists to provide and of the welfare society exists to ensure. The individual thus possesses the ultimate autonomy, since he is the end to which both state and society are means.

To this point, no American liberal could disagree. However, Morton went on to define Canadian political culture in a way that distinguished it from American liberalism.

But that autonomy carries with it a sovereign obligation to respect and safeguard the autonomy of his fellows, primarily by manners, which are the dealings of man with man, and secondarily through the social and political order. So reciprocal and delicate a complex of justice, welfare and good manners may function only in an organic unity of state, society, and individual. It was such a unity of king, church, and people Canadians, both French and English, inherited from their remoter past and have elaborated in their history as a monarchical and democratic nation.

This was a concise statement of Canadian conservatism, but by 1971 Morton saw his vision of Canada under attack from three directions. He published a second edition of his book with a new chapter: "Canada under Stress in the Sixties" (University of Toronto Press, 1972). In it, he described the conversion of Quebec from a Catholic to a materialistic and secular society, and the corresponding rise of separatism; the decline of Britain in the world and as "the exemplar and inspiration of Canadian life"; and the danger that U.S. business investment in Canada would lead to U.S. economic control. Morton warned that Canada's distinct society had been created by history and was dependent on tradition:

In a traditional society, society governs, and its members find themselves by serving that society. In that fact exists at once the weakness and the strength of Canada. Not for it the simple ethics of the joint-stock state, a limited agency for the collective realization of individual right, and the pursuit of profit as the chief end of man. But if in a traditional society, becoming in fact ever more populist and pluralist, the tradition were not transmitted, the society would perish; *only if it is transmitted from generation to generation can Canada survive.* (Emphasis added)

In search of what remained of Canadian conservatism, Charles Taylor, a Red Tory writer, interviewed Morton shortly before he died in 1980, and found him sanguine about the future of the country and the ability of conservatism to adapt to changing circumstances. However, it is hard to believe that were Morton alive today he would still be optimistic, for the conservative tradition has not in fact been transmitted to the modern generation. The danger he saw in the 1960s has become if anything more threatening. Quebec nationalism has grown stronger, few Canadians are any longer conscious of Britain as a model, and integration with the U.S. economy proceeds apace.

What explains the decline – indeed, disappearance – of the conservatism that was influential for so many centuries and was supposed to be Canada's secure foundation? George Grant thought that it had been dead, or at least dying, even before Confederation. In his stimulating essays on *Technology and Empire* (Anansi, 1969), he pointed out that free thought in the eighteenth century, in what was called the Age of Enlightenment, had challenged all established wisdom, and that the rise of science and the Industrial Revolution seemed to offer limitless possibilities. In this age of change, liberalism was the rising ideology, and it defeated conservatism so completely that now we can hardly comprehend a society based on conservative values. Technology meant not only new machines and inventions but also new ways of thinking, and in the modern world the universal goal was to build a society of free and equal individuals. This was liberalism, and it caused us to forget what we lost in the age-old conservative vision of human society. "All coherent languages beyond those which serve the drive to unlimited freedom through technique have been broken up in the coming to be of what we are," Grant wrote, adding, "it is just to pass some antique wind to speak of goods that belong to man as man." In *Lament for a Nation*, he said:

> The history of conservatism in Great Britain has been one of growing emptiness and ambiguity. A political philosophy that is centred on virtue must be a shadowy voice in a technological civilization. When men are committed to technology, they are also committed to continual change in institutions and customs. Freedom must be the first political principle – the freedom to change any order that stands in the way of technological advance. Such a society cannot take seriously the conception of an eternal order by which human actions are measured and defined.

In Grant's bleak view, British conservatism was already a spent force when Canadians adopted it as their ideology, and this doomed Canada as a country both independent of the United States and distinctly different. "The impossibility of conservatism in our era is the impossibility of Canada," he wrote. "As Canadians we attempted a ridiculous task in trying to build a conservative nation in the age of progress, on a continent we share with the most dynamic nation on earth. The current of history was against us." The British model, he argued, could provide us with parliamentary and judicial institutions different from, and better than, those of the United States, but not with a different way to organize our industrial society. With such an analysis, it is no wonder that

Grant gave his book the subtitle *The Defeat of Canadian Nationalism*. But many have read his pessimistic analysis as a warning rather than a final judgment on Canada.

Robert Stanfield, when leader of the Conservative party, was foremost among the more practical politicians who believed not only that the conservative model remained valid in Canada but that it was probably vital to the survival of the country. At a special meeting of his Opposition parliamentary caucus on 20 November 1974, he set out his views on conservatism (heading his notes, with typical dry humour, "Not to be quoted or used against me"). Referring frequently to the British tradition, he identified the central principle not as freedom of enterprise but as "the importance of order, not merely 'law and order,' but social order." Conservatives, he went on, believed that a decent civilized life required a framework of order, a quality quite rare in the world, and they were prepared to impose restrictions on private enterprise to preserve it. In the 1974 election, Stanfield had translated the principle into policy by proposing to fight inflation by freezing incomes and profits. That earned him the support of the *Toronto Star,* usually a social democratic newspaper, but upset many Conservatives who thought of their party as the advocate of free-enterprise capitalism. It also opened him to attack by Prime Minister Trudeau, who mocked the idea of a freeze but later introduced his own version of income and price controls, and by the New Democrats speaking for the labour unions, which opposed a freeze on wages. The result was a Liberal victory and eventually Stanfield's resignation as party leader – perhaps the last Conservative leader to articulate a truly conservative outlook. "The emphasis on the nation as a whole, on order, in the conservative tradition that I have described, was surely seldom more relevant than it is today, with inflation raging and life becoming more and more a matter of every man for himself and the devil take the hindmost," he told his caucus, continuing:

> We see increasing stresses and strains in our society, wildcat strikes, increasing distrust and mounting tension and violence. This is a period when true Conservative principles of order and stability should be most appealing. Principles of conservation and preservation are also high in the minds of many Canadians today, and a Conservative can very legitimately – and on sound historical grounds – associate with these ... Enterprise and initiative are obviously important, but will emphasis on individual rights solve the great problems of the day? I mean the maintenance of acceptable stability, which includes price stability, acceptable employment, and an acceptable distribution of income. Would we achieve these goals today by a simple reliance on the free market, if we could achieve a free market?

Stanfield's question was rhetorical and his answer obviously no. He has been called "the best prime minister we never had," but had he won office would his ideas have been acceptable in modern Canada? Probably not, and it is perhaps more appropriate to call him, with affection and respect, the "Last Conservative." His successor, Joe Clark, was described as a Red Tory, but showed little evidence of interest in that philosophy before he was swept away by Brian Mulroney, who seemed to have no fixed beliefs.

George Grant was surely right in attributing the defeat of conservatism – and, in his view, of the original conception of Canada – to technologies which have opened to us a seemingly limitless future, accelerated the rate of change, and thus swept away the idea of an eternal order that was the foundation of conservatism. Our mind-sets have changed. To point to a few specific examples of how technology has changed Canada, consider transportation, communication, and climate control in homes and offices. At Confederation, most Canadians were of British or French stock, and European ideas and values were bred into their bones in a Christian country with two major cultures. (At that time the cultures of the aboriginal peoples had no influence on the white society.) Air travel, particularly the jumbo jet, has changed all that. We are today a multicultural society with growing numbers of people of African, Asian, and Hispanic stocks, and of many different religions. Even if they wish to assimilate to Canadian values, the old conservatism can mean little to them. The Mountie, once the icon of Canadian conservatism, may now wear a turban.

In communication, television leads the way in creating a new and constantly changing popular culture. It also dominates politics, and frequently questions the legitimacy of the government. This style of journalism reflects a liberal, and therefore American, mistrust of the state and all its works. In short, and for better or for worse, TV is inconsistent with the idea of an orderly and stable society with fixed values and an accepted hierarchy. Margaret Atwood and others have argued that the Canadian national character is formed in part by the struggle for survival in a hostile natural environment. However true this may have been in earlier times, it can hardly be a factor in the age of central heating, air conditioning, instant snow removal, automobiles that insulate us from the weather, and airliners that shrink distance.

"Deny the legitimacy of ideology and you deny men a particular meaning to their own collective history," wrote Herschel Hardin in his much-admired book *A Nation Unaware* (J.J. Douglas, North Vancouver), published in 1974. "The disintegration of identity follows, and has followed in Canada." But the ideology on which Canada was founded has not been denied to us; it has been outmoded by change. Conservatism is impossible in a world swept by change.

CANADIAN VALUES

History has left us, if not with a distinctive ideology, at least with an idea of qualities we like to think of as being Canadian. Numerous attempts have been made to describe them, and so to define the Canadian identity. The most elaborate, ironically, is by an American sociologist, Seymour Martin Lipset, in *Continental Divide: The Values and Institutions of the United States and Canada* (Routledge, New York, 1990). He surveyed history, literature, political and economic behaviour, cultural achievements, religious traditions, and public opinion polling data to discover and describe the ways in which Canadians differ from Americans. It is not a criticism to say that he starts with the obvious which we have already discussed. Any search for Canadian identity must start with the founding values, and Lipset writes:

> The very organizing principles that framed these nations [the U.S. and Canada], the central cores around which institutions and events were to accommodate, were different. One was Whig [British liberals of the seventeenth and eighteenth centuries] and classically liberal or libertarian – doctrines that emphasize distrust of the state, egalitarianism, and populism – reinforced by voluntaristic and congregational religious tradition. The other was Tory and conservative in the British and European sense – accepting of the need for a strong state, for respect for authority, for deference – and endorsed by hierarchically organized religions that supported and were supported by the state.

Lipset found the influence of those ideologies still alive, but diminishing:

> I am not trying to suggest that America and Canada are still Whig and Tory societies in the late 18th-century sense of these terms. Canada obviously no longer approves of hierarchy and rule by the elite; it has increasingly accepted the individualistic values and some of the institutions derived from the [U.S.] Revolution. The United States ... has long since given up its unwillingness to use government to deal with social and economic problems or to recognize group rights and needs as distinct from those of the individual.

Canada has moved even closer to the U.S. model, he argues, by adopting the Charter of Rights and Freedoms, with its emphasis on protection of the individual and on judicial supremacy. But "in spite of this and other changes, Canada, as we shall see, remains more respectful of authority, more willing to use the state, and more supportive of a group basis of rights than its neighbour." As evidence, he cites the existence of social democratic parties in

English and French Canada (the New Democratic Party and, presumably, the Parti Québécois, although its ideology is now doubtful), our extensive welfare state, state ownership, the strength of trade unions, and the constitutional rights given to French Canadians and ethnic groups.

These are familiar themes in the considerable literature on the Canadian identity. So also are the claims that we are more orderly and peaceful than Americans (our rates of crime are lower, for example) and more tolerant of minorities, as evidenced in our commitment to bilingualism and multiculturalism, both controversial ideas in the United States. We like to think of ourselves as peacemakers rather than warmongers, compassionate and ready to share the national wealth rather than greedy, profit-driven individualists. All these virtues which we claim for ourselves can be questioned. For example, Allan Gregg, the pollster, and Michael Posner, a journalist, point out in their book *The Big Picture* (Macfarlane Walter & Ross, 1990) a portrait of modern Canada based on social surveys: "On the one hand, we believed we were more tolerant than Americans – that Canada was what President George Bush had in mind when he said he wanted to make the United States a kinder, gentler nation. On the other, the reported incidence of rape and violent assault, racism and illegal drug use had reached levels once associated with the inner ghettos of American cities ... More and more, our inner cities are populated by those who can't afford to leave, the very rich and those who work for the rich." To take another example, public support for bilingualism has been declining, and the Reform party owes some of its support to the fact that, alone among national parties, it rejects the idea of Canada as a partnership between two founding peoples, French and English. It seems to call for unhyphenated Canadianism, just as many Americans reject multiculturalism and demand unhyphenated Americanism distilled in a melting pot.

In other words, Canada may not so much be different from the United States as a few years behind it. The rapid changes in the make-up of the population produced by immigration, the integration of the two economies that was under way long before it was ratified by the Free Trade Agreement, and the continentalization of entertainment, including sports, must all whittle away differences in values. Lipset acknowledges the argument but insists that differences remain – while conceding that they are mostly a matter of degree. Others continue to find distinctive Canadian values. As the chairman of the Citizens' Forum on Canada's Future, Keith Spicer, wrote in 1991:

> Having criss-crossed this country in every direction, and met people
> of every origin and status, in large towns, tiny hamlets and farms, I
> find a deep similarity of values and ideals among Canadians ...
> Freedom and dignity in diversity, with openness to all cultures and

races; a sensitive democracy; a clean environment; the often unspoken idea of North; a peace-supporting, more independent role in an increasingly interdependent world; a yearning to love this country in any way each individual chooses, without apology – the right to be a Canadian in different ways, times and places, or not very much at all.

The report of Spicer's commission was a little more precise and summarized Canadian values under these headings:

- Belief in equality and fairness in a democratic society
- Belief in consultation and dialogue
- The importance of accommodation and tolerance
- Support for linguistic, regional, ethnic, and cultural diversity
- Compassion and generosity
- Attachment to Canada's natural beauty
- Commitment to freedom, peace and non-violent change in the world

The federal government adopted this definition of Canadianism in its 1991 plan for constitutional reform (*Shaping Canada's Future Together*) and proposed to elaborate them in a symbolic "Canada Clause" in a renewed constitution to supplement what is now essentially a legal document. "All Canadians," it said, "should be able to relate to the description of the qualities that define the country to which they are bound by birth or choice." That would have surprised the Fathers of Confederation, who thought they had adequately defined Canada as similar to the United Kingdom, and in a sense it moved us closer to the United States with its statements of founding values and governing principles.

Some of the qualities that the government thought made up the "Canadian identity" could equally well have described the American identity, but others certainly would not. The U.S. constitution emphasizes individual rights, but the Canadian draft, while reaffirming the rights of individuals set out in the Charter of Rights and Freedoms, added group or community rights. The Canada Clause was to recognize, among other things:

- "that the aboriginal peoples were historically self-governing ... and their rights within Canada;
- "the responsibility of governments to preserve Canada's two linguistic majorities and minorities;
- "the special responsibility borne by Quebec to preserve and promote its distinct society."

The clause also implied social and economic obligations for governments when it recognized:

- "A commitment to the objective of sustainable development in recognition of the importance of the land, the air and the water and our responsibility to preserve and protect the environment for future generations"; and
- "A commitment to the well-being of all Canadians."

This inclusion of collective rights and duties was no accident. The Canada Clause, the government said, should embody "the balance that is especially Canadian between personal and collective freedom on the one hand and, on the other hand, the personal and collective responsibility that we all share with each other." The Conservative government's constitutional proposals, including the definition of Canadian identity, were endorsed by the Liberal and New Democratic parties, business and labour leaderships, and by most of the mass media, reflecting at least a consensus of elites on Canadian values. They were then rejected in a referendum, partly because the majority declined to be tolerant by recognizing Quebec's claim to be a "distinct society" within Confederation, leaving the national identity as much in doubt as ever.

Before it was rejected, the Canada Clause seemed to express the old conservative, or Red Tory, view of society, and to reinforce other conservative values already in the constitution: the emphasis on peace and order, and the recognition of the supremacy of God. But in addition it was optimistic and activist in spirit – in a phrase, social democratic rather than conservative. We have already pointed to the similarities between conservatism and social democracy, and Lipset also makes that case: "To reiterate a key point, there is good reason to believe that social democratic movements are the other side of statist conservatism." Canadian Toryism, he suggests, has mutated into social democracy, and he is surely correct. Horowitz ended his essay on Red Toryism saying something similar: "A tory past contains the seeds of a socialist future."

As Canadian liberalism long ago became social democratic in practice, and the NDP and the Bloc Québécois are officially social democratic, this is now the dominant Canadian ideology. Reform is harder to classify, but is probably best located on the right of the social democratic spectrum. I do not argue that the parties are identical, only that they operate within the same framework of values, with differences of degree rather than of principle, differences in policy means but not in social ideals. Similarly, although the United States has modified its original liberalism by recognizing group rights – for example, in employment equity programs – and by looking to government for economic and social leadership, its model of social democracy is far from identical with the Canadian model. But the differences between the two societies are not ideological, as they were in 1867, and it is probably true to say that most English-speaking Canadians feel more at home in the U.S. than they do in French-speaking Quebec.

POPULAR CULTURE

We hear constantly that we must protect and promote Canadian cultural industries – principally publishing, film, television, music, and theatre – so that our artists can articulate the Canadian identity. But as we no longer have a distinct political and cultural identity, that notion can lead only to frustration and failure. It is more sensible to accept that popular culture has become international, as high culture always has been. High culture is essentially European in origin, and while popular culture is usually described as American, it owes a great deal to Afro-American influences and to immigrants forced by anti-Semitism and other horrors to transport their artistry from Europe to the United States. Popular culture is American in the sense that it reflects the suffering, turmoil, and energy of the New World – and, perhaps most important, because it is mass-produced and marketed as entertainment by American technology and business methods.

These commercial products dominate consumer markets for entertainment around the globe, and national popular cultures, so-called, are essentially branch plants. They copy the American products, sometimes making minor changes to acknowledge their own national experience. When Canadian films and TV programs are made to international standards, when Canadian musicians achieve excellence, when our actors and artists rival or exceed the best in other countries, they contribute to international culture, sometimes with a noticeably national or regional flavour which we recognize with pleasure. We can and should support the cultural industries in the same way that we support other key industries, but they do not and cannot express a distinct national culture or identity.

CONCLUSION

The crisis of social democracy is for Canada much more than a problem of politics and economic management. It is a crisis of national identity. We no longer have a distinctive national ideology or culture that transcends regional differences to create identity and bind the country. If the country is to survive, we have to reinvent it, and that will require finding answers to hard questions we would rather leave unasked, and reaching agreement on the difficult changes that are necessary. To do that we need at minimum an efficient and democratic system of government, and that's the subject of the next chapter.

CHAPTER FOUR

The Failures of Our Federalism

We should expect three things from a system of government. It should be democratic, which is to say that it should be seen to reflect the will of the majority, and thereby command at least the respect of dissenting minorities. It should be economical and efficient in operation. And it should enable us to respond quickly to new threats and opportunities in a fast-changing and unpredictable world. Our model of federalism – Confederation – and the parliamentary system of election and governance meet none of these requirements. It is therefore not surprising that Canadians are cynical about politics and politicians and feel they have lost control – which indeed they have. Nor is it surprising that we are finding it hard to adjust to changing economic and social conditions.

The view that we should forget about the constitution and focus on the economy is woefully misguided. The constitution specifies how our system of government is to work, and government plays a leading role in economic affairs. If our system of government does not work well, it is unlikely that the economy will prosper – unless we are prepared to rely mainly on market forces. Markets certainly change fast, ruthlessly discarding the old and rewarding the new, but the social cost is often high. Whole industries can be devastated, whole economic regions undermined, throwing thousands into unemployment and some into poverty. That's not acceptable in a democracy; people demand that their government somehow protect them from disruption of their lives. Usually, they want the government to reverse change and return them to what in retrospect look like the good old days, but that is not possible. The best that governments can and should do is to maximize the benefits and minimize the costs of change.

They can assist industries to adapt to change, and provide financial and other support – for example, retraining – to people who are displaced by economic change. They can also negotiate economic agreements – for example, trade deals – with other countries to manage change so that it occurs by agreement over time and is not violently disruptive. But while measures of this type are easy to conceive, they are often difficult for democratic governments to implement in time to be of much use. The reason is that in a large modern democracy like Canada change that makes one citizen richer will make another poorer, at least in the short term. Worse, what is good for one community or even for one economic region is bad for another. For example, in the last century the wrongly named National Policy imposed tariffs on foreign goods to protect manufacturing industries in central Canada. Central Canada was happy, but it was bad for the West, which had to pay high, protected prices for manufactured goods while selling its own primary products at unprotected world market prices. The West could do little about the tariff policy because central Canada elected more members to the federal Parliament. This became a major source of western alienation, which has remained potent to this day.

Economic change creates conflict also at the social or class level. To survive, business leaders must respond quickly to market forces, and the most enterprising among them even welcome the challenge of change as an opportunity to grow and make more profit. But workers often believe that they have more to lose than to gain from change, and it is true that the skills and seniority they have acquired in one industry are often not transportable to a new one. In a rational world they would understand that change is unavoidable and in fact the only way in the long run to raise living standards, but it is human nature to deny even the obvious when it is threatening. And it is all the easier to deny it when there are politicians insisting that the changes are the fault of an evil government serving somebody else's interests. Thus governments when they propose change find themselves the target of hostility from many conflicting interests, and unless they can build a national consensus for action, they often find it easier to do nothing. This is generally true in all large democracies, but let us now see why it is particularly true in Canada.

CONFEDERATION

To understand the problems of Confederation we have to consider briefly its origins and development. It grew out of the failure of the Province of Canada, the union of Upper and Lower Canada (which we now know as Ontario and Quebec) in 1840. While they had an equal number of seats in the legislature, the two Canadas had quite different ideas on religion, education, and other issues, and in each there were conservative and liberal parties. In those divisive circumstances it was difficult for any party or alliance to form a stable government. By 1864 the legislature was deadlocked: in a period of a few months there were four governments, some lasting only a day or two. Meanwhile, the threat from the United States seemed to be growing and the ability of the British government to protect its colonies was declining, suggesting to the Canadians that they had better look to their own security. At home, farmers and merchants in growing Ontario were eager to expand westward, thereby breaking out of the straitjacket which the equal partnership of the two existing Canadas imposed. Then occurred perhaps the greatest act of statesmanship in Canadian history. The liberal leader in Ontario, George Brown, editor of the powerful Toronto *Globe,* rose above his bitter political and personal differences with the conservative leader, John A. Macdonald, and offered to join a coalition government under Macdonald if it would seek some form of federal union of the British colonies in North America. Macdonald jumped at the chance offered by his old enemy, Quebec conservatives approved, and soon talks were begun with the Atlantic colonies. By 1867 the deal was done, separating Ontario and Quebec but making them provinces, with Nova Scotia and New Brunswick, in the new Canadian Confederation.

It was far from a deal made in heaven, as Macdonald freely admitted when urging the old legislature of the two provinces to accept the Confederation plan:

> I have always contended that if we could agree to have one government and one parliament legislating for the whole of these peoples, it would be the best, the cheapest, the most vigorous and the strongest system of government we could adopt. But, on looking at the subject in the Conference, and discussing the matter as we did, most unreservedly, and with a desire to arrive at a satisfactory conclusion, we found that such a system was impracticable. In the first place, it would not meet the assent of the people of Lower Canada [Quebec], because they felt that in their peculiar position – being in a minority, with a different language, nationality and religion from the majority – in case of a junction with the other provinces, their institutions and their laws might be assailed and their ancestral associations, on which they prided themselves, attacked and prejudiced ... We found, too, that ... there was as great a disinclination on the part of the various Maritime Provinces to lose their individuality, as separate political organizations, as we observed in the case of Lower Canada itself. Therefore, we were forced to the conclusion that we must either abandon the idea of union altogether, or devise a system of union in which the separate provincial organizations would be in some degree preserved. So that those who were, like myself, in favor of a legislative union were obliged to modify their views and accept the project of a federal union as the only scheme practicable.

Macdonald, however, was nothing if not a crafty politician, and the scheme of Confederation adopted was neither truly federal nor unitary. To use his words, it was in some degree one and in some degree the other, and even the term Confederation was misleading. In a confederacy, independent states agree to form a union but hold strongly to their separate identities, assigning to the central government only limited powers. In forming a federation, independent states surrender the principal powers to the new central government and retain sovereignty only over matters of local concern. Macdonald said the Canadian plan reserved to the federal parliament "all the great subjects of legislation," while the provinces were given control "of all local works" and the local taxes needed to finance their own development. But just to make sure that the provinces did not get too ambitious, the federal government had authority to disallow provincial legislation. Thus the Fathers formed a federation but called it a confederation, and there was a large measure of ambiguity in the plan from the outset.

But despite this attempt to have the best of both worlds, there was little enthusiasm outside Ontario. In Quebec, Confederation was opposed by liberal reformers. In both Nova Scotia and New Brunswick there were powerful, at times majority, anti-Confederation movements. Prince Edward Island originally said no but finally joined in 1873, pushed by Britain and offered a financial bail-out by Ottawa. Newfoundland did not join until 1949, and then with reluctance. The expansion westward was no more glorious. The territories that now make up most of the Prairie provinces were originally granted by the Crown to the Hudson's Bay Company as a private trading preserve, and at Confederation were bought back for cash and land grants and made part of the new Canada. When the local inhabitants, the French-Indian Métis, decided they would rather have their own state and rebelled, they were suppressed by Canadian and British troops, and their leader, Louis Riel, was hanged, in the worst colonial tradition. British Columbia was not at first inclined to enter Confederation but was persuaded to join in 1871 by the promise of a railway to link it with the East, which then took some fifteen years to build.

Thus Confederation was the result not of vision or of political ideals but of a crisis which undermined the old order, and a series of deals made by political leaders without much reference to the wishes of the people. Some of the deals were based more or less on promises and payments to hard-up colonial governments, and the division of powers was at best ambiguous and at worst a deception. The whole shaky structure has been kept alive by almost endless negotiation between the central government and the provinces. Indeed, the British North America Act had hardly been proclaimed when the provinces began to quarrel with Ottawa about the distribution of powers and revenues. They were soon arguing for a broad interpretation of their powers as enumerated in the BNA Act, and the final court of appeal – at that time the

Judicial Committee of the Privy Council in Britain – tended to agree with them. By broadening the powers of the provinces, the judgments reduced those of Ottawa and changed the balance of power within Confederation. As the historian Creighton later wrote, "It was no longer possible ... to look on the provinces as subordinate, semi-municipal bodies" – which had been Macdonald's conception of the role they should occupy. The late Senator Eugene Forsey, a prolific and respected authority on the constitution, argued for years that the Judicial Committee wrecked Macdonald's grand design. The other point of view is that Macdonald's centralizing plan had never been workable and that the judges reinterpreted the BNA Act to hold the country together.

Among other factors that have eroded Ottawa's jurisdiction and empowered the provinces has been simply the growth of government into areas which the Fathers never foresaw. When Macdonald reserved for Ottawa what he considered the great areas of policy, health and social welfare minor matters and were left to the provinces. Now they are among the most important functions of government. At Confederation, education was tied to religion, mainly Catholic in Quebec and Protestant or non-denominational elsewhere, and so had to be a provincial jurisdiction. Now it is one of the main activities of government. Thus the responsibilities of government have shifted so far that it is fair to say that the provinces have within their jurisdiction many of the matters of most concern to the voters. But Ottawa has not been willing to accept this situation and has found various ways to overlap the provinces, usually by using its superior taxing power to bribe the provinces to do as it wishes. For example, health insurance, or medicare, is clearly a provincial jurisdiction, but Ottawa got around that by offering to pay each province half the cost of operating a plan that met Ottawa's specifications. The offer was particularly attractive to the poorer provinces because it meant that Ottawa would tax the people of wealthy Ontario and transfer the cash to them. In similar ways, Ottawa bribed or pressured the provinces to introduce other national programs. The point is not whether the plans are good or bad, but that they could be achieved only by bending the constitution.

Ottawa's superior taxing power itself resulted from yet another ambiguity in the BNA Act. At Confederation the principal sources of revenue were indirect taxes such as customs tariffs, and Ottawa took those – adding prudently a catch-all clause providing that it could raise money by "any Mode or System of Taxation." The provinces were granted only direct taxes, which meant mainly property taxes. But then income tax was invented, making direct taxation the greatest source of revenue. The provinces had the right to use this rich direct tax but Ottawa had the same right under its catch-all clause. The result has been frequent bickering and overlapping taxes. Both levels of

government tax the same citizens – or, rather, overtax them – but Ottawa
hands billions back to the provinces in grants and subsidies of one kind and
another. One example is the equalization formula under which Ottawa in
effect transfers revenues raised in the richer provinces to governments in the
poorer provinces, to ensure a basic level of public services across the country.
At first sight this is just and, indeed, said to be a pillar of Confederation. But
the result is a national levelling down. The rich provinces reduce their own
incomes to pay a permanent dole to their poorer partners, which are kept in a
style they can't afford. They are far from prosperous, but not so poor that their
citizens have to accept that the local economy cannot support them and move
to where opportunity is greater – as of course their forefathers did in coming
to Canada in the first place.

After decades of such wheeling and dealing, federal-provincial fiscal relations are so complicated that only a handful of civil servants and possibly a
few politicians understand them. Collectively, the provinces now spend more
than the central government, and borrow huge amounts at home and abroad.
They regulate sections of business, write much of the labour law, and exercise
powerful influence on trade policy. Nevertheless, Ottawa is supposed to manage the national economy by raising or lowering taxes and spending, and by
controlling the money supply. There is of course much talk of federal-
provincial co-operation, and hundreds of meetings are held every year, from
the highest level, the heads of the eleven governments, down to officials. But
while almost every federal prime minister starts off by promising to get on
with the provinces, in the end there is always conflict. Perhaps the most
obvious but least important reason is that four or five parties are usually represented in the eleven governments and a certain amount of partisan point-
scoring is inevitable: it may not be serious but it does not improve the atmos-
phere for negotiation. Second, when things go wrong, as they often do, the
two levels of government try to escape responsibility by blaming each other,
further confusing the public.

These problems alone would justify a reorganization of our federalism,
but there is in addition the problem of Quebec and the danger that it will separate, thereby ending Confederation as we know it, plunging us into a constitutional crisis, and possibly even into violence. Conciliating Quebec has therefore been the preoccupation of most federal prime ministers, and they have
been encouraged in this by the fact that the people of Quebec have usually
been smart enough to win powerful representation in the federal government
by voting as a bloc for the party likely to win in an election. In fact, it is
unusual for any party to form a majority government in Ottawa without winning the majority of seats in Quebec. It follows that Ottawa gives enormous
attention to Quebec's problems, seeking always to make the province happy

with special administrative arrangements, or by plans to change the constitution to recognize the province's special place in Confederation. This is of course infuriating to much of the rest of Canada, particularly the West, where the French language and culture are only weakly represented.

The basic problem is probably beyond solution within Confederation because English- and French-speaking Canadians have fundamentally different views of the arrangement. To generalize, English-speakers have shared Macdonald's vision of a strong central government with overriding power to make policy for one nation from sea to sea. French-speakers, on the other hand, have always regarded Confederation as a compact between two equal nations, French and English. This Two Nation version of history is not supported by a strict reading of the BNA Act, but it has had some recognition in practice. The Liberal party has alternated its leadership between English and French. In the national government English and French are equally official languages, and until quite recently, when multiculturalism became fashionable, it was customary to talk of two Canadian cultures. It is not surprising therefore that the Québécois refuse to accept the idea that Confederation was intended to create one Canadian nation with an English-speaking majority. For them, it is a partnership and should allow them to preserve their own distinct nation. Their national assembly is in Quebec City, not Ottawa, and they are always suspicious that the federal government is encroaching on the social and cultural powers awarded to them in the BNA Act, thereby threatening their national identity.

Quebec's nationalism was not a serious threat as long as it remained inward-looking and accepted the conservative leadership of the Roman Catholic Church in social affairs. Its governments resisted federal encroachment mainly by refusing to co-operate with national plans. But in 1960 a new Liberal government came to power determined to use the power of the provincial state to modernize the society. This was indeed a Quiet Revolution, as it came to be called, and to carry out its ambitious plans the government needed all the powers awarded to it in 1867, and more. These demands for powers and revenues brought it into conflict with Ottawa and at first outraged most English-speaking Canadians, who had, during the Second World War, come to accept the leadership of the national government even in social and cultural affairs. However, the constitutional force of Quebec's case was hard to deny and other provinces began to realize that they too could make good use of the powers and revenues Quebec was demanding.

English-Canadian nationalists opposed to U.S. influence in Canada admired, even envied, the force and conviction of Quebec nationalism. So there was in the 1960s, at least among political, intellectual, and media elites, a growing acceptance of the idea that the best solution for Canada would be some form of what was called "special status" for Quebec within Confederation – in other words, a Two Nations concept. The Liberal government in Ottawa appointed the Royal Commission on Bilingualism and Biculturalism and drifted toward special status by conceding powers and revenues to Quebec. The NDP made special status part of its official policy. The opposition Conservative party accepted a Two Nations approach at the same national convention at which it rejected the leadership of John Diefenbaker, the prairie populist who insisted on speaking of "One Canada." Of course, the vision of One Canada was still in the hearts of millions of English-speaking Canadians who resented Quebec's threats to national unity, but Diefenbaker had proved a failure as prime minister and was no longer a credible spokesman for the cause.

But then, from Quebec itself, a credible spokesman emerged, Pierre Trudeau. An opponent of any form of nationalism based on ethnic identity, he opposed special status because he believed it would lead inevitably to the separation of Quebec from Canada and the creation of a closed society in which all except the Québécois would be second-class citizens. The noble attempt to create in Canada a state able to accommodate two nations would have failed, and French-speaking Canadians outside Quebec would soon be assimilated into the English-speaking majority. So instead of a Two Nation Canada, he offered the concept of One Nation with two official languages and cultures. Instead of two solitudes there was to be one country sufficiently bilingual and bicultural to be equally accessible to all Canadians. It was a fine vision – with immense appeal to millions of English-speaking Canadians as long as the emphasis was on One Nation. But the notion of two cultures was not attractive to the growing population of new immigrants who were neither French nor English in heritage and preferred a policy of multiculturalism in which French culture would be only one among many minority cultures. Bilingualism was soon seen by many if not most Canadians as another concession to Quebec, and also financially wasteful. In practice, few English-speaking Canadians were willing and able to learn French well enough to live and work in the language, and while many Québécois were fluently bilingual, few wanted to live outside their own province – which became increasingly unilingual in French.

Thus Trudeau's policies failed to reconcile the English and French Canadas within the framework of Confederation. Attempts to solve the problem by amending the BNA Act were no more successful. Some changes were accepted by Ottawa and the English-speaking provinces but rejected by Quebec; others were accepted by Ottawa, Quebec, and some of the other provinces, but rejected by public opinion in English-speaking Canada, mostly because they seemed to confer a form of special status on Quebec. Predictably, the Québécois responded by saying that if they could not achieve what they considered a satisfactory position within Confederation, they wanted out. According to opinion polls, most want political sovereignty for Quebec and an economic association with Canada rather than outright independence. Sovereignty-association is of course just another if rather extreme form of the Two Nations/special status concept, and so we are back to where we were in the 1960s. The past thirty years have been a diversion, an enormous waste of political energy on an attempt to evade the real problem: that the existing Confederation cannot be made acceptable to both the English-speaking majority and the French-speaking minority.

To sum up this review of Confederation as a form of federalism, it fails on several grounds. It encourages overlapping and therefore wasteful government. Because the division of powers between federal and provincial governments is so complicated, it is almost impossible for voters to know which politicians are responsible for what and to hold them accountable. It provides no central point at which all the powerholders are required to agree on and abide by national policies. Rather than uniting French and English, it tends to divide them. And finally, simply keeping the structure standing absorbs enormous amounts of political energy. In short, it is no way to run a country when the requirement is for fast response to a changing world by efficient government that commands the informed support of the public.

PARLIAMENT

If the Canadian constitution was at best ambiguous, the British model of parliamentary government that the Canadians so unthinkingly adopted also had large elements of smoke and mirrors. In the same year as Confederation, 1867, Walter Bagehot, founding editor of a famous British periodical *The Economist,* described the workings of the British government as he observed it as a journalist rather than as a political theorist or philosopher. His book, *The English Constitution,* became a classic and is still in print. He saw that the parliamentary system was in reality a disguised republic. The Crown, the House of Lords, all the pomp and ceremony, were what he called the "dignified" elements and served mainly to impress the uneducated working classes, who were unable to appreciate the subtle mechanisms of democracy. As he remarked, you could hardly expect your servants to understand such matters. In practice, power was in the hands of a cabinet of ministers drawn from the House of Commons, in turn drawn largely from the middle class, practical men of affairs – the "efficient" element in the British system in Bagehot's analysis.

It is ironic to note that Bagehot did not recommend this deceptive arrangement to "the North American colonies of England." Here, he thought, people were better off and better educated than in Britain and therefore quite capable of running their own affairs without a "dignified" element to command awe and obedience. Despite that good advice, the monarch was, until quite recently, revered in Canada as the supreme ruler by divine appointment, and a royal visit was a cause for national celebration. In the absence of the monarch, the governor general, often a British aristocrat, was a figure of ceremonial importance and occasional political influence. For the sophisticated there was the argument that the Crown was a brilliant constitutional device, a figurehead of state standing above the politicians, ensuring the continuance and legitimacy of the state even when things went horribly wrong, and facilitating the orderly and peaceful transfer of power.

This justification for what is obviously an archaic system is still advanced, although many democratic republics survive and manage the transfer of power quite well without a monarch. In any event, the role of the "dignified" elements in the parliamentary system has become increasingly irrelevant in Britain, and in Canada both the monarchy and the office of governor general have lost much of their status. The Queen is respected as a person, even loved by some, but is not seen as a ruler. Her family are treated as celebrities rather than leaders or role models, and increasingly act the part. Governors general are hardly visible and rarely of political account. To the extent that the monarchy has been part of Canada's political culture, its decline contributes to our crisis – to the sense that we are losing our distinct identity. Even *The Globe and Mail*, the champion of the monarchy in Canada until quite recently, now says it should end with the present queen and be replaced with a governor general chosen by distinguished citizens.

Another "dignified" element in the British system was the House of Lords – the Upper House of Parliament, so called, in which sat the lords temporal, who were the aristocrats and landowners, and the lords spiritual, the bishops of the established church, together representing two estates of the realm. (The third estate was represented in the lower house, or House of Commons.) In his *Dictionary of Political Thought* (Macmillan Press, London, 1982), the British scholar and writer Roger Scruton says that in the "Westminster model," as copied in other countries, the upper house is structured "so as to embody the dignity and durability of the state and of the interests within it, but with limited legislative power, consonant with its non-representational character. Normally the upper house would be thought of as a revising chamber."

This is what the Fathers of Confederation had in mind when they created the Senate. It was supposed to represent the interests of the provinces and of the propertied class – one of the qualifications for membership was owning real property worth at least $4,000 – by taking a "sober second look" at the legislation proposed by the elected House of Commons where democracy might become mob rule. Partly because prime ministers have often chosen to put their friends and allies into the Senate, it has not enjoyed the confidence of the provinces, so failing in one role. But as many senators have been company directors, it has certainly on occasion protected private business interests. Rather unfairly, the Senate has become a target for unceasing attacks by the media, which do not understand its role in the Westminster system we adopted, and it has become an object of contempt, regarded as a plush rest home for worn-out party hacks. If there is one issue in the constitutional debate on which almost all Canadians agree, it is that the Senate ought to be abolished or made more "efficient." In other words, we wish to remove another "dignified" element in the parliamentary system, a foundation stone in the model which the Fathers of Confederation so readily copied.

What about the "efficient" element, the House of Commons? The historic achievements of the Commons in Britain were to wrest autocratic power first from the Crown and then from the lords, and to establish a form of government by consent of the middle class. MPs were prominent local citizens. They organized loosely in parties based on different conceptions of the national interest – for example, free trade versus tariff protection – and they chose their own leaders in the Commons. But they also represented the interests of their constituencies, at least as perceived from the manor house or the counting house, and were prepared on occasion to dismiss a government formed by their own party and install another if they thought it desirable. With the Industrial Revolution, public education, the widening of the franchise, and the organization of mass parties, MPs came to represent different classes and ideologies rather than local constituencies, and the Commons in this century has been a forum for a non-violent class war.

The Conservatives, by and large, represented the well-to-do and tradition, the Labour party the less-well-off and a new vision of society. It was efficient in the managerial sense: one party usually had a majority of seats in the Commons and could form a cabinet, which in effect ruled by decree. Debate about the cabinet's proposals was not intended or expected to change them in any significant way. The business of the opposition was not to participate in government or to seek a compromise, but simply to oppose – to discredit the government if it could, and to offer the voters an alternative program based on its own ideology. Only in times of great national danger, such as war or economic catastrophe, did the competing parties agree to adjourn the ideological battle and join in what was usually, and revealingly, called a National Government – as opposed to sectional or class government. Nowadays, with the decline of ideology as a distinguishing mark in politics, the party battles are mostly sham, and there are frequent attempts to form third parties committed to open government, genuine debate, and compromise. They fail, largely because governments formed by the established parties have so far refused to change an archaic system of election: a separate contest in each constituency in which the candidate with the largest share of votes wins, even if that share is far less than 50 percent. The result is that the party which forms the government often has the support of only about 40 percent of the voters. In the 1992 election, for example, the Conservatives under John Major won with 42 percent of the vote, with 58 percent voting for opposition parties, mainly of the centre-left. This was hailed as a triumph for Conservative party ideology, although it was obviously nothing of the kind.

The advantage of this crazy system for the two major parties, Conservative and Labour, has been that it is hard for a new party to win a significant number of seats and become a serious competitor for power. The disadvantage is that politics, which is to say the democratic process, falls into disrepute, as the Labour party seems now to recognize, since it proposes, when and if in power, to reform the method of election. But this is the system we have slavishly copied in Canada. The results are even worse than in Britain. Ideology has not been important in our politics because divisions are usually between economic regions and the cultures they shape, and between groups based on cultural identity, rather than between classes. If conflicts can be resolved, at all, it is only by compromise. The regions need to see that their points of view are expressed in the national legislature and taken into account by government, that their language, cultures, and customs are represented and respected when national policies are made. If there has to be a compromise, they have to understand what they are getting and giving, and why.

As this sort of debate and negotiation almost never occurs in the Commons, new parties spring up to elect MPs to speak in Ottawa for parts of the country that feel they lack influence at the parliamentary centre of power. They usually fail because Parliament long ago ceased to be the centre of power – it may in fact be just as alienated from power as the regions it fails to represent. In times past, in Canada as in Britain, MPs were notable citizens only loosely organized in parties. They chose a leader who, when the party won the largest number of seats in the Commons, became prime minister. The prime minister chose a cabinet of ministers, which had to include regional party chiefs with powerful followings of their own, sometimes former provincial premiers. He also had to keep a wary eye on his backbenchers, who were only part-time politicians, had deep roots in the constituencies in which they lived, and might or might not vote as he desired. John A. Macdonald called such independently minded MPs "loose fish," and several times, to his irritation, saw them defeat his government's legislation in the Commons.

Party leaders of course played a leading role in politics, but they were "the first among equals" rather than supreme commander. All is now changed. The party leader is chosen not by MPs but by a national party convention, a device we copied from the vastly different U.S. system of government. Few of the ministers have any personal following, and on becoming prime minister, the leader hires and fires at will, favours or disciplines backbench MPs to ensure their obedient votes in the Commons, and controls the national party organization mainly by dispensing patronage. He or she is the ruler of cabinet, caucus, and Commons. Policy is made in private by the prime minister and the cabinet, and if there are objections from backbenchers they are discussed in private in the caucus. True, public debate in the Commons follows, but since everyone knows that it will not change government policy, it is barely reported in the news media. Thus regional protest parties are excluded from power even when they elect MPs, as they did in 1993.

Not once since the Second World War has a party won a majority of the vote in a national election. In 1984 the Conservatives did get as high as 50 percent and they were rewarded with 75 percent of the seats in the Commons. The other 50 percent of voters who supported mainly the Liberals or the New Democratic Party were supposed to be content with 25 percent of the seats and no role in government. In 1988, Conservatives won with only 43 percent of the vote, but that was enough to gain them 57 percent of the seats. The 57 percent of voters who supported candidates who were not Conservative managed to elect only 43 percent of the MPs who were condemned to the sterile role of opposition. The results of the 1993 election were even more outlandish. With 41 percent of the vote the Liberals gained 60 percent of the seats. The Reform party won 19 percent of the votes and 18 percent of the seats, while the Bloc Québécois with fewer votes (13.5 percent) got more seats and became the official Opposition. The unfortunate Conservatives won 16 percent of the vote and less than 1 percent of the seats, while the New Democrats got fewer votes (7 percent) and more seats (3 percent).

Almost all modern democracies have adopted some form of proportional representation. That is to say, seats in the legislature are divided between the parties in proportion to the support they receive from the voters. Canada, because of its slavish adherence to the Westminster model, is one of the few countries with a system of election that usually disregards the wishes of the majority of voters. This perversion of democracy is justified in the name of strong government. The argument is that the parties put their programs before the electorate, and the party that wins a majority of seats can drive its legislation through Parliament and be held accountable for the results at the next election. However, as we know too well, parties are often elected on one program but find in power that it is impracticable, or that circumstances have changed and demand different priorities.

As Prime Minister Trudeau said during the 1968 election campaign when he was accused, incorrectly as it happened, of having no specific program, politicians cannot foresee what problems they will face in office. Using the examples of the era, he pointed out that U.S. President Lyndon Johnson had been elected to create the Great Society and instead escalated the war in Vietnam, while British Prime Minister Harold Wilson promised a white-hot technological revolution and wound up negotiating an austerity program with the conservative International Monetary Fund to secure support for the pound sterling. Trudeau, it can be added, promised a Just Society but was diverted by economic crises and constitutional issues, supporting his point that voters should choose a leader who seems to them to have the right attitude and approach, rather than a detailed program that may never be implemented. Brian Mulroney declared himself an opponent of free trade when he campaigned for election in 1984, then proceeded to negotiate a deal with the United States, and considered it ratified when he won 43 percent of the vote in 1988.

In practice, modern elections are usually a contest between images of leadership created by party machines and the media, rather than between programs. Voters choose a leader, although of course we do not do anything as sensible as letting them vote for a leader. In theory they vote for a local MP; in fact they usually vote for the party of their chosen leader, further undermining the idea that MPs represent their constituency in Parliament. Then our system gives the winning leader power to legislate as he or she chooses, without regard for the opposition parties, which almost always represent the majority of the voters.

We should note in passing that while claiming to be a parliamentary democracy we have in fact abandoned one of its central principles – the supremacy of Parliament and the belief that the best and final protectors of the freedoms of the people are their elected representatives. By adopting the constitutional Charter of Rights and Freedoms, we have limited the role of Parliament by specifying areas in which it may not legislate, and we have transferred to the courts the power and responsibility to settle many basic questions about our society. Given the failures of our system, as noted above, the Charter may be not be a bad idea, but it further undermines the parliamentary form of government.

Is it any wonder that voters are alienated from the political process at both federal and provincial levels? We tolerate the parliamentary system only because it is familiar, allegedly part of our national identity and beyond critical examination. But if we were designing for ourselves a new system of government – as the Americans, the Germans, the Japanese, the Russians, and many other countries have done – and one among us suggested our present system, he would be laughed out of the room, and probably right into an asylum for the insane. We can't now build a sensible democracy by fiddling with what we have. We need to start again from fundamentals, and perhaps to look for models to countries more modern and successful than Britain.

THE MEDIA

Journalists cannot be blamed for the failures of our federal system, except perhaps to the extent that they have been slow to discover and report on its fundamental flaws. But journalists have certainly contributed to the decline of Parliament. They have usurped the role of the opposition in the Commons, setting themselves up as the real critics of the government. And they have transferred public attention from national parties, which used to be the forum for policy formation, to pressure groups, which pursue a single cause with religious zeal that makes compromise difficult to achieve.

The press of course has always been a political institution. Many papers were set up in the nineteenth century to support a party, Liberal or Conservative, and it was not unusual for an owner/editor to be also an active politician. But with the spread of education and literacy and the invention of the high-speed press, mass-circulation papers became possible, and so profitable that they no longer needed subsidies from the parties. Publishers, wanting to appeal to as many readers as possible, declared their political independence, claiming to be objective reporters of the facts, without fear or favour. In reality, press and party allegiances continued in Canada until at least the 1950s. In Toronto, for example, the *Star* was generally Liberal and the *Telegram* fiercely Conservative. (*The Globe and Mail* was pro-business, switching its support from Conservative to Liberal depending on which seemed most favourable to business at the time.)

In this partisanship the reporters in the parliamentary press gallery reflected the struggle between the government and opposition on the floor of the Commons, and were in a real sense a Fourth Estate – or, as Prime Minister William Lyon Mackenzie King put it, an adjunct of Parliament. The tradition was different in the United States, where the division of political power was not between government and opposition but between three branches of government, the presidential executive, the legislative Congress, and the Supreme Court. By providing that the Congress could not limit the freedom of the press, the U.S. constitution implied that the press was a sort of fourth branch with a mission to keep a watchful eye on the other three – to serve, as it were, as an additional check and balance.

In the 1960s a momentous change occurred. Canadian journalists shook off not only party ties but also the notion that they were merely neutral observers of events. They began to think of themselves as guardians of the public interest as they defined it. Instead of focusing on the debate between government and opposition in the Commons, they assumed the task of investigating and auditing the work of politicians and of exposing their failings when they did not meet the expectations of the media. They thus became a Fourth Estate outside Parliament, in the U.S. rather than the Canadian tradition, often adversaries of the elected politicians.

Several factors combined to bring about this change. One was that the idea of objective journalism had always been something of a fraud. Reporters and editors had to make subjective judgments about what to report and how to report it, based on the commercial need to entertain as well as the duty to inform readers – and sometimes, of course, influenced by a hidden political agenda. This was apparent to many young journalists emerging from the tumultuous universities of the 1960s and '70s. To them, the claim to objectivity was hypocrisy: the media were obviously serving the established commercial and political elites. They wanted to be social reformers and approached all institutions with cynicism. Two young journalists in Washington showed what could be achieved by reporting the Watergate affair and helping to overthrow a president. Another major factor was the rise of television journalism, which packaged news as dramatic entertainment, often focusing on personalities in conflict and injecting the on-camera reporter into the middle of the story. Unable to compete with radio in speed of news delivery, or with TV in dramatic impact, the press turned on the one hand to muckraking and on the other to serious analysis and commentary, sometimes in the same paper.

A third factor, probably, was that the failings of parliamentary government, as described above, were becoming apparent, causing journalists to abandon the press gallery in favour of "scrums" and more formal press conferences in which they competed with politicians to set the public agenda. A minor but interesting example of the new, proactive journalism occurred during the 1993 election when the CBC decided that ordinary Canadians felt excluded from the political process. In the past, it might have reported on this phenomenon so that the parties could, if they wished, correct the situation, but now it decided itself to correct this defect in the system by inviting ordinary voters into its studios where they could confront the politicians.

But in general, reporting of the Commons declined sharply in the 1970s and '80s, making a bad parliamentary situation worse. However, the politicians and others found new ways to get their messages to the public through a screen of journalists who wished to control the public agenda. A pioneer in this field was Abbie Hoffman, the U.S. hippie leader who announced in his book *Revolution for the Hell of It*, "We have learnt how to manipulate the media." The secret was simple: package your message as an exciting news story and hungry journalists would carry it to millions. For example, he called a news conference to announce the formation of a non-existent youth party, and invited young people to meet and demonstrate around the Democratic party convention in Chicago in 1968. For journalists, the formation of a political party was news as they understood it, and they carried the story across America. The result was chaotic violence in the streets of Chicago which rocked the mighty Democratic party. Similarly, the FLQ crisis in

Quebec in 1970 was a made-for-the-media event which succeeded to a dangerous extent in destabilizing Canada. Scores of other groups have used similar manipulative but more peaceful methods to attract media and public attention to such causes as native rights, abortion reform, protection of the environment, and labour disputes. Noisy demonstrations with simple messages provide more entertaining news than party conventions debating policy issues, seeking compromises among competing regional and commercial interests, and passing resolutions which governments may or may not implement, and so the national parties have lost much of their legitimacy. Faced by journalists who are intensely sceptical if not downright hostile, politicians far more than in the past employ experts to communicate to the public via the mail, by advertising in the mass media, and by stage-managing "photo opportunities" and news conferences, which the media feel bound to cover as news.

The Committee of Inquiry into the National Broadcasting System, appointed by the Canadian Radio-television and Telecommunications Commission, summed up the new attitude of journalists in a 1977 report:

> Those who work in these [news] media feel, rightly, they have heavy social responsibilities, and they tend to regard themselves as forming a much more effective form of opposition to a government than any political party with the second largest vote can ever exert. They feel they are the real source of informed criticism, the only means through which major scandals like Watergate can reach the public, the only means of arousing the public to a sense of concern. As an opposition, they feel privileged and like all institutions, they tend to identify the welfare of society with the preserving of their privileges. A democracy based on open debate cannot reject such a role, however self-appointed, much less try to curtail or suppress it. Still, it is a political role, and the vast majority of politicians find sooner or later that they are following public opinion much more than they are leading or guiding it.

Practised by well-informed and responsible journalists, the new journalism of analysis and commentary can be fair, balanced, and more informative than the old. Practised by those for whom "a good story" takes precedence over the facts, or who arrogate to themselves the task of opposing the elected representatives, it can be destructive of the democratic process. As we move toward direct democracy in the form of extended national debates and referendums on major issues, the role of journalists becomes more influential and that of elected politicians less. In retrospect, there is much to be said for the party journalism of years ago when readers knew the ideological bias of a paper and more than one interpretation of the news was readily available. We may return to something like that if newspapers in their current format find it impossible to compete with electronic media. But for the present we have to live with what is in effect a new branch of government tacked onto the parliamentary system.

BUT IS CANADA REALLY AS BAD AS ALL THAT?

The reader is entitled to ask at this stage, "But if our system of government is such a mess, why have we been so successful as a country? How did we achieve a high standard of living, a relatively peaceful society, and a social safety net much superior to that in the United States?" The blunt answer is that in the long view Canada has not been a particularly successful country. Prior to the Second World War, by most accounts, we were a cultural backwater with a primitive economy. We looked to Britain for leadership in political affairs and increasingly to the U.S. for social and cultural ideas. Our economy, based on the export of raw materials to technically advanced industrial countries, suffered cruelly during the Great Depression, and there was nothing we could do about it. English and French co-existed as two solitudes in one country, and the native peoples were dismissed as second- or even third-class citizens.

The Second World War was Canada's opportunity. Far removed from the fighting that overran and largely destroyed the European powers and Japan, we rapidly industrialized and found ready markets for everything we could produce in the new factories, on the farms, in the forests and fisheries. Hundreds of thousands of Canadians marched off to war, and for many of those who survived, military service was a better life than the unemployment and poverty they had suffered at home. And for Canadians who remained at home it was a time of progress and prosperity. Canada emerged from the war, which destroyed most of the prewar Great Powers, as an economic and even a military Middle Power, a neighbour and ally of the United States, which the war had made a Superpower. We were rich and influential and this happy state of affairs tended to overshadow internal divisions and discontents.

By the 1970s the world was changing again. Europe and Japan had rebuilt themselves and were challenging the economic supremacy of North America, and new economic powers were emerging, principally in Asia. Times were no longer as comfortable for Canada and consequently prewar divisions were reasserting themselves. Most Canadians would agree that our economy is now in difficulty, partly of our own making, and we maintain our standard of living only by borrowing from foreigners. The social security system in which we take such pride is threatened. We have failed to resolve the English-French division, and the strains on Confederation, or national unity, are probably greater than ever before. In short, we enjoyed about thirty years of success as a country, 1945–75, and are now face to face again with our underlying problems.

CHAPTER FIVE

WHAT'S TO BE DONE?

We have in the preceding chapters discovered the roots of Canada's problems in the crisis of social democracy, in the failure of our federalism and our parliamentary form of government. In sum, our problems are systemic – that is to say, they are inherent in our system and we cannot solve them merely by electing a new prime minister at the head of a new government. We have to change our system of governance, review and probably change the way in which governments operate, and reform our social and economic policies.

It's a daunting task and prompts the question of how to begin, or to put it another way, What's to be done? As some will recognize, the question is adapted from the title of a famous book by Lenin, who thought he knew the answers, but the purpose here is to learn from his mistakes. In that slim volume he denied that the socialist revolution would emerge naturally and inevitably from the workers exploited by capitalism, and argued that at least in Russia revolution would have to be led by an elite of professional revolutionaries. This "rock hard" elite, mostly intellectuals to whom Communist ideology was a revealed truth beyond debate, would be the vanguard of a mass party of workers. While Lenin's ideas on organization and leadership made possible the Communist seizure of power in Russia – and were later imposed on Communist parties around the world – they were also, arguably, the explanation of the Soviet Union's rapid descent into tyranny. The idea of a broadbased and essentially democratic movement had been compromised, and the absolute power of the ruling elite led to absolute corruption.

The lesson is that radical change is likely to succeed only when it is generated and monitored by the democratic process and is seen to enjoy majority support. It is one thing therefore to make the case, as I have done, for radical change in the Canadian system, but it would be presumptuous and a profound mistake – a sort of Leninism – to dictate what the change should be. If solutions are to work they must emerge from democratic debate and decision. It is for Canadians to invent the New Populism – that is, decide how best to regain control of their politics, how to make government work for them so that they can lead change instead of being dragged behind it, and so become victors rather than victims in the new global economy.

In the past we left the definition and solution of problems to our own elites, the politicians we elected and their professional advisers, the bureaucrats, with the academics and journalists in supporting roles. Indeed, that's the process prescribed by our parliamentary form of government: we elect representatives to manage our affairs more or less as they think best, and review their record only every few years. That's how we got Confederation, and it's how we have since tried to correct its deficiencies. Our heads of governments have met at countless constitutional conferences, agreed reluctantly that there are problems and that something must be done, and proposed numerous solutions. They have even gone through the motions of consulting the people by appointing parliamentary committees and task forces to hold public hearings. And some of their suggestions have been passed into law by some of the parliamentary legislatures, usually over the objections of opposition parties. But the mass of Canadians were not deeply involved until all eleven governments agreed upon the Charlottetown formula for change and submitted it to the people in a referendum in 1992. Whereupon the people said no.

It would be wrong to assume that all those who voted no were rejecting the Charlottetown accord on its merits, or even objecting to the way in which it was reached by negotiation among the elites. Many were expressing their anger at governments in general and the Mulroney government in particular because of the failure to solve economic problems. Others objected mainly to what they interpreted as concessions to Quebec, which they believed would give it a status superior to that of other provinces. But the 1993 election showed that there was tremendous dissatisfaction with the political structure and method of government operation. A post-election study of the vote revealed that more than half of those who voted in 1988 and again in 1993 changed parties, an astonishing and unprecedented level of volatility. Nevertheless, the system produced a majority Liberal government which promised not change but a return to the good old days, and it excluded from power new parties proposing change.

CHANGING THE SYSTEM

Most Canadians will probably agree that in order to regain control of government we need to reduce it in size and complexity. We can do that in two ways. One is to change the structure of our federalism so that government is smaller and closer to the people. The second is to change the way in which government operates. Let's deal first with changing structures. It is now generally accepted that if we are to reform Confederation – change our defective system – there is no going back to the old ways of decision-making by elites – what political scientists call elite accommodation. The elites failed in the task of producing a Charlottetown settlement acceptable to a majority of Canadians.

On the other hand, it is unrealistic to think that a cohesive and comprehensive package of reforms to the system can arise naturally from ordinary people busy with their daily lives, not well informed on the basic constitutional issues, and not much interested in what they regard as abstract constitutional problems. We do not expect the voters at election time to invent a detailed program for government to follow. We offer – or purport to offer – several programs and ask the voters to choose. To reinvent Canada we must adopt a similar procedure. The Citizens' Forum therefore was only a start on a process that now urgently needs to be continued. As the commissioners said in their report: "On many specific dilemmas facing Canadian government and society, no one yet has detailed answers. Certainly we do not. Many of these demand expert advice and research, and far more time than the eight months we had ... We were not charged with reinventing federalism or rewriting the constitution."

Yet reinventing federalism is what needs to be done. The first task is to define the problems more clearly, explain the costs and benefits of alternative systems, and put them to Canadians in a way that requires hard choices rather than general expressions of hopes, prejudices, and uninformed opinions. Defining issues and explaining possible solutions is a job for experts. Debating, perhaps improving, and choosing among solutions is a job for the people, and the essence of a New Populism. What's to be done here is to suggest the questions that need to be asked, the range of possible answers, and a process to make it all happen.

DO WE NEED TO CHANGE AT ALL?

A debate on fundamentals must be prepared so that we can think about what some will say is unthinkable – for starters, whether Canada is a viable national state in the changing world. When the Bloc Québécois became the official Opposition in the Commons last year, there were loud protests precisely because the party argued that Confederation had failed and should be dissolved. So let us first deal with the notion that merely to question the viability of Canada is treason, or at least a betrayal of the national legacy. Of course it is not. Dissent by lawful means is the life force of democracy, and it includes the right and sometimes the duty to challenge in Parliament or elsewhere even the fundamentals of the country. After all, as we have seen, Confederation itself grew out of the failure of an earlier model of Canada. If Confederation is failing, it is the highest form of patriotism to face that problem and find solutions.

In fact, although national states such as Canada may seem to us to be the natural and best order of things simply because they are familiar, in historical perspective they are forever changing. A few centuries ago there were hundreds of separate nations of aboriginals on the North American continent. Using superior technologies to defeat them, the Europeans absorbed the aboriginal nations into French, English, and Spanish colonies. Next, new technologies of transportation and communication in the last century – notably railways and telegraphs – tied these colonies into three national states, Canada, the United States, and Mexico, by centralizing political and commercial power and homogenizing cultures.

As yesterday's technologies created national states, today's are creating superstates. The North American Free Trade Agreement aims to create a continental economy, and the treaty undeniably creates a degree of continental government. Similarly, across the Atlantic the European Community, now known as the European Union, is gathering national states into a continental superstate.

So no matter how much we may be attached to present arrangements, change is inevitable. At one level continental consolidation is under way, but at another level there is a process of disintegration within national states – a return to the identities that existed before the states were formed, and a flow of power from national to regional governments. Here in Canada, Québécois and aboriginal peoples are seeking some degree of independence. In the West there is a strong sense of regional identity and alienation from the centre. TV journalist Eric Malling reported in his "W-5" program (CTV, 31 March 1994):

Say the word "constitution," and most of us hear "Quebec." For decades now the leaders of that province have argued that Canada might work better with less federal government ... Well, the argument always gets tied up in language and culture, and usually ends in name calling. But guess what? Listen today and you hear a lot of the same things from the other side of the country, in British Columbia. No one talks seriously about separatism, but B.C. is booming these days. It already has a separate economy, and maybe some different arrangements with the rest of the country could make it even better off, and a lot happier.

Interviewed by Malling, Rafe Mair, former provincial politician and now an influential broadcaster, suggested the choice for British Columbia in the future was probably going to be between a "renegotiated Canada" and a closer association with adjoining U.S. states – a concept which already has a name, Cascadia, and even a flag.

Even Ontario, which has been proud to think of itself as a heartland of

Confederation, is now complaining about the amount of wealth that the federal government transfers from it to poorer provinces. The last several federal governments have accepted the need to surrender spending power to the provinces to allow them more autonomy. In the United States, the notion of a cultural melting pot is seen increasingly to be a myth, or at least a pot that works only for whites of European descent. Afro-Americans and Hispanics in particular claim their own cultural identities, and indeed legal and illegal immigrants from Mexico are on the way to regaining control of the vast territories seized from Mexico by the United States in the last century. The devolution of power from Washington to the states has been called the second great revolution in American federalism. In Western Europe, the United Kingdom is becoming less united, as Scotland and Wales each seek some degree of autonomy. There are similar tendencies in other developed democracies.

(The story is quite different in other parts of the world in which both economies and democratic ideas are underdeveloped. Some former colonies seem to be reverting to a primitive tribalism. Others seem still to be in the process of forming large and stable national states in which industrialization can proceed. The lesson may be that, in any society, democracy and the rule of law evolve over many years, perhaps centuries, and cannot be transferred by an imperial power to a less developed colony.)

The formation of superstates and a return to regionalism or ethnic identity are not contradictory but complementary. Both replace national states. As globalism saps the power of national governments to manage the economy within their borders, they lose a major reason for their existence. The binding power of national identity based on common economic interests and distinct national cultures declines. People begin to question the purpose of the national state in which they live – as they are now doing in Canada. But the alternative, continental or global identity, remains amorphous, so people return for a sense of belonging to ethnic and regional loyalties.

We tend to view the decay of the state in which we live as a disaster. For example, at the time of Confederation many people living in the Maritimes, Quebec, and Ontario were opposed to surrendering their colonial identities to create a Canadian state. But changing states and national identities is not necessarily a bad thing. In the global economy, breaking up a large federal state and returning to more regional identities may be economically advantageous. In his new book *Global Paradox* (William Morrow and Co., New York, N.Y., 1994), trend-watcher John Naisbitt says, "The bigger the world economy, the more powerful its smallest players." And it is true that the fastest-growing economies have been such small states as Singapore, Hong Kong, and Taiwan. The explanation may be that in a rapidly shifting global economy the countries that do best are those that can respond fastest to external market changes.

To respond fast requires consensus on policy, which can be achieved only if there is a high degree of social cohesion. Small countries – and those, like Japan, with a unifying cultural identity – are cohesive. Big countries spanning many regional economies and including many ethnic minorities are not cohesive because there are too many competing interests. Instead of making national policy and acting on it, we argue about who will win and who will lose. What's good for the West may not be good for Ontario, and vice versa; and our political processes allow protracted and frequently inconclusive negotiation.

In the era of national economies serving national markets, size was an advantage. Now it may be a disadvantage. This is an argument for reorganizing large countries like Canada; to refuse to contemplate such changes, even though such a stance may seem patriotic, is to put the country at risk. We are not talking here about abolishing national states as we know them. With so much history behind them they will not swiftly disappear and no doubt will continue to play a leading role in international affairs. But we should consider how we can best organize our states, and begin to think in different ways about nationality and citizenship. Indeed, we are already thinking continentally in our economic and cultural lives. In an article on "Redefining Sovereignty for the 21st Century," an unusual team of American and Canadian writers suggested, "We might, in the near future, see ourselves as Quebecers or Californians, as 'East Coasters' (for want of a better term) or Pacificans (equally infelicitous), and as North Americans on top of all that – all depending on which issues and which constituencies we are dealing with at the time." (The authors of the article are Stephen Blank, director of Canadian Affairs at the Americas Society in New York, Marshall Cohen, president and CEO of the Molson Companies Ltd., in Toronto, and Guy Stanley, who was then a visiting professor at L'Ecole des hautes études commerciales, in Montreal: it was published in *The American Review of Canadian Studies,* 1991.) In other words, we may identify with different political states for different purposes.

The first question therefore answers itself. Canada as we know it will not survive. Change is unavoidable, and the real question is whether we shall welcome and manage the process or wait for events beyond our control to force it upon us with results we may not like.

WHAT ARE OUR OPTIONS IN DESIGNING A NEW CANADA?

In reforming the system of government the first choice is the one they faced in 1867 and then dodged, between a unitary and a federal state. As we have seen, John A. Macdonald favoured a unitary system with one strong central government for all Canada, but the Maritimes and Quebec objected. The outcome was a compromise, called a confederation but actually, as we have seen, a federation. We need now, in changed circumstances, to review and perhaps change that compromise.

The obvious advantage of a unitary system would be that it would eliminate one whole level of government, the provinces, or at least reduce provinces to an administrative role. There would be national policies for all, an end to federal-provincial fights over jurisdiction and tax revenues, and in theory at least administration would be streamlined and costs reduced. But the objections would surely be stronger today than they were in 1867. The original objections were to a loss of local identity based on history and custom, but economic imperatives were driving in the other direction, toward the formation of large states. Today, as we have noted, the trend is to return from national to local roots.

It is also an undeniable fact that government has become a vast undertaking and is beyond the effective supervision of any one legislature. Even when power and responsibility are divided between two levels of government there are frequent complaints that the federal or provincial parliaments are not dealing with this or that issue, that there is insufficient time for debate on legislation, and that bureaucrats and the courts rather than MPs are allowed to make policy. Above all, there is the sense that a remote central government is insensitive to local concerns. If responsibility for all the activities of government were to be concentrated in one parliament in far-away Ottawa, all these problems would necessarily be worse.

An alternative to a unitary system would be a more genuinely federal system. This could take one of a number of forms. We might for example choose a congressional form with the federal power divided between a prime minister nationally elected to represent the national interest, a senate representing the provinces, and a house of commons representing the voters in their constituencies. Or we could look at the German model in which the regional states are directly represented by delegates in one of the two chambers of the central parliament. The federal parliament makes policy but its laws are largely administered by the states.

Another option would be to form what we claim already to have, a confederation. (As a reminder, states forming a federation surrender most of their powers to a superior level of national government, which is what happened in 1867. In a confederation, the states assign to the national government only limited powers and retain a large measure of autonomy.) The result would be to reduce very sharply the powers, duties, and size of the central government. A true Canadian confederation might be formed by the ten provinces and two or three territories as we know them, but it would probably be more practicable to base it on four or five regions. Ontario, Quebec, the Atlantic region, and the West might be the regions. Or perhaps the Prairies and the Northwest Territories would make one region, with British Columbia and the Yukon forming another. It might also be practicable to create for the purposes of government an additional region to represent self-governing aboriginal communities.

The regions or provinces would be sovereign except to the extent that they assigned powers to a central government, presumably in Ottawa. The idea would be to limit central powers to those necessary to manage the union, thereby allowing to the provinces or regions the maximum freedom to run their own economic, social, and cultural affairs in accordance with custom and democratic decision. Two obvious questions arise. How would such a small central government be appointed, and what powers would it have? It might be appointed by a parliament directly elected across Canada, as we have today. But that would be to set up once again two parallel structures of government, one national and one provincial or regional, with all the possibilities for political competition and wasteful overlapping from which we now suffer. In such a confederation, the regional or provincial governments would be senior and would probably wish to assign to the independently elected centre only the minimum necessary jurisdiction. These might be trade and other relations with foreign countries; national defence; immigration; monetary policy and the currency; criminal law; the Supreme Court to resolve constitutional disputes and administer, among other matters, the Charter of Rights and Freedoms; and the raising of revenues required to finance just those activities.

An alternative to an elected national parliament might be a central administration run by delegates appointed by elected governments in the provinces or regions. In such a system the provinces or regions would collectively control the central administration and might therefore be willing to expand its mandate to include programs of social and economic development. Such a confederacy would be similar to the European Union in which national states meet at the centre to agree on community policies, which bind them all. True, there is a European parliament whose MPs are elected and are independent of national governments, but the real power seems to reside with the national governments meeting in council, and with the international commission they have created.

To use another analogy, it would be a form of sovereignty-association for all provinces or regions, not just Quebec. And why not? We should at least consider whether a Canadian union that would satisfy Quebec might also be good for other regions. A decentralized confederacy run by the provinces or regions might look attractive to most Canadians – when they got over the shock of the new. It would eliminate the unfairly elected and ineffective federal Parliament and slash the vast federal bureaucracy; a slimmer administration with limited powers and lower costs would take their place. Because the central authority would be weaker, the peoples of the provinces or regions, with their different economies and customs, would have more latitude to decide how to organize their affairs. With different economic, social, and cultural policies, the provinces or regions would compete with each other and learn from each other. Political debate and responsibility would be focused at one level of government, close to the voters, where social cohesion is likely to be stronger than at the federal level and consensus easier to find. Issues of concern to all the provinces or regions would still be dealt with at the centre, including broad economic issues such as the choice between free trade and protectionism.

Some of the national symbols would probably be discarded, leaving it to each province or region to decide whether it wished to be a monarchy or a republic, to have a parliamentary or a congressional form of government, to be officially unilingual, bilingual, or even trilingual – with no federal presence to overshadow local distinctions. We could expect provinces or regions to accelerate the process, which is already under way, of strengthening ties with neighbouring U.S. regions, thereby moving toward a North American confederation. National programs such as old age pensions and unemployment insurance, which are supposed to unite all Canadians with their federal government, might be replaced by provincial or regional schemes suited to local needs and finances. And there would probably also be less willingness by Canadians in the wealthy regions to pay subsidies to those in the poorer regions. But such measures have not in the past produced national unity, and they may in fact retard economic restructuring in depressed regions. Conversely, a union of more functional democracies and more efficient local economies might strengthen pride in and a commitment to a new Canadian confederation.

Many other models of federalism and confederalism could be devised, and in fact federal and provincial governments in Canada have been talking for years about changing their areas of jurisdiction to make the system more efficient. But the basic flaw is never addressed: while responsibility for economic management is in Ottawa, much economic power is decentralized to the provinces. This a recipe for irresponsible government, waste, and overlapping. A new system of government should, at the minimum, match power with responsibility, and that would probably mean ending the sovereignty of either the federal or provincial level of government.

DIRECT OR REPRESENTATIVE DEMOCRACY?

Whatever federal or confederal structure we favour, there is a basic choice to be made between direct and representative democracy. In a direct democracy the people come together to make their own decisions about public policy. In small communities in the past, for example, they held town hall meetings, discussed the problems, and decided on the solutions by majority vote. But this was obviously impracticable in large provinces and even less workable when a whole country was involved. The solution was a system in which people elected a representative to travel to the provincial or national capital, put their point of view, and vote on their behalf. The representatives were often prominent citizens who were better educated than those they represented, and better informed on national issues because in the capital they heard many points of view. The idea developed therefore that representatives had a higher duty than merely speaking and voting as their constituents directed. They were to speak and vote as they thought best in the provincial or national interest, and because that would be good for the province or nation it would ultimately be good for their constituents also. If their constituents did not agree with the judgments made by their representative, they could remove him or her at the next election.

Representative democracy worked well enough in the past but there seems now to be an interest in returning to some form of direct democracy. This is probably because Canadians are better educated and better informed on affairs by modern mass media. New forms of instant communication – television in particular – suggest the possibility of holding community meetings for an entire province or even a whole country. U.S. populist leader Ross Perot, for one, proposed if elected president to govern by holding national "town hall" meetings on TV in which he would consult the people. The CBC in last year's election staged "town hall" meetings in which representative members of the public questioned candidates, and the rest of the electorate were invited to participate by viewing the exchanges before deciding how to vote. Going further, the CBC provided panels of voters with electronic gadgets on which they could register their instant reactions to political messages. Call-in shows on radio and TV are another medium through which people participate directly in national debates. The Reform party wants to introduce a degree of direct democracy by giving voters more control over their MPs, and by referring some major issues to the people by means of referendums.

The referendum on the Charlottetown accord was an example of direct democracy and attracted a high level of public interest and involvement. The elected representatives prepared the accord but then asked the people to discuss it at length and vote yes or no. The people voted no and thereby rejected the judgments of their representatives. We have to wonder, however, to what extent most Canadians want to participate directly in government on a regular basis – and whether they are prepared to do the work required to participate responsibly. Governments make decisions every day, and MPs and members of provincial legislatures spend a great part of their time studying issues on which they must eventually vote. With a living to earn and perhaps a family to raise, the average citizen does not have the time or the interest to be constantly involved in government decision-making, but she or he probably does want to be consulted more frequently and effectively than in the past. This will require a major change in our system, which has been almost entirely representative, with infrequent recourse to referendums for such fundamental issues as changing the constitution.

HOW SHOULD GOVERNMENTS BE ELECTED?

Whatever structure of government we choose – unitary, federal, or confederal – we should look carefully at the various systems for electing our governments. But surely we would not confirm our present arrangement. Many better models are available, and the choice will depend to some extent on the form of government. The U.S. congressional system, for example, has obvious flaws but it does require agreement between the president, who is elected to represent the nation, the senators, who represent the people in their states of the union, and the congressmen, who represent the people in their districts, or constituencies. Decision-making is often messy and protracted, but it is far more open and participatory than the Canadian system. It is sensitive to a fault to local and regional concerns, and this explains why party discipline is weak.

The handling of the NAFTA issue provides a useful example of how the Canadian and U.S. systems differ in operation. In Canada NAFTA was driven through the Commons by a Conservative government at the end of its term over the objections of the opposition parties, some of the provinces, and the majority of the people speaking through opinion polls. In the United States, President Clinton had to negotiate with individual members of the Congress to secure support, and while he was criticized for "buying" votes by promising government aid for constituencies, the voters could see what was being traded in each deal. The outcome of the long struggle, in doubt until the end, was probably as good an expression of the national will as could be achieved.

In Europe most democracies have some form of proportional representation which ensures that the representation of parties in the legislature reflects more or less the wishes of the people as expressed in the vote. This often means that no single party has a majority, making a coalition of two or more parties necessary. Each party in the coalition may speak for an ideology, a region, or even a religious point of view, but they are forced to compromise to find the best common expression of the will of the nation. Again, decision-making may be protracted, and there may be frequent changes of government, but it would be hard to prove from the record that such governments are less successful than Canadian governments.

Indeed, the Task Force on Canadian Unity, in its 1979 report, declared that our electoral system was corroding national unity because "the simple fact is that our elections produce a distorted image of the country." It proposed to modify the imbalance in the Commons by adding sixty seats, to be awarded to the parties in proportion to the votes they received. No action was taken despite the fact that the Task Force was chaired by two pillars of the political establishment, Jean-Luc Pépin, a Liberal, who had held several federal cabinet portfolios, and John Robarts, former Conservative premier of Ontario. The report was signed by others hardly less distinguished, including academics, politicians, and a labour leader. The NDP leader at the time, Ed Broadbent, later suggested implementing the Pépin-Robarts proposal, and Prime Minister Trudeau indicated he would assent if the Conservatives agreed. Conservative leader Joe Clark dissented, and that was that. Considering that last year they won 16 percent of the vote, but less than 1 percent of the seats in the Commons, the PCs may think that Clark made a mistake. Under the proposal, they would have won twelve seats. The Royal Commission on Electoral Reform and Party Financing, appointed in 1979, had a broad mandate but decided for some reason that it was not supposed to consider such a basic reform as proportional representation – without which nothing else much mattered.

The usual argument against proportional representation is that it would encourage minor parties and probably elect a House of Minorities – a legislature in which there would be no majority party to form a stable government. In other words, if Canadians were allowed to elect the representatives they really wanted, it would turn out that there was no consensus on who should govern or what should be done, and there would have to be real debate, compromise, and perhaps even trade-offs between competing interests to win majority agreement on a legislative program. What a shockingly democratic idea!

A less shocking way to improve the electoral system would be what is called the single transferable vote. Voters rank candidates in the order of their preference, for example making the Liberal their first choice, the New Democrat their second, the Green candidate their third, and so on. All the first preferences are counted first, but if none of the candidates has more than 50 percent of the total, second preferences are allocated. This continues until one of the candidates has more than half the votes and is declared elected with the closest possible approximation of a majority mandate.

Our present system is biased to elect governments with the support of less than half the voters. Once in power, in Ottawa or in a province, these governments rule more or less as they wish, ignoring other parties and the majority of voters who support them. Any electoral system that compelled parties to compromise and form coalition governments would be more representative, and would encourage more open debate and greater public participation in decision-making.

CHANGING THE WAY GOVERNMENTS OPERATE?

The second way in which we can reduce the size of governments and bring them under better control is to change the way they operate. We look now to government both to make policies and to implement them through an army of slow-moving civil servants – or too often through bureaucrats who are less than civil and far from servants because they administer regulations we cannot understand. It doesn't have to be this way. We can restructure governments so that they function as policy-makers and regulators but farm out operations to business and to non-profit community organizations. An influential guide to how this can be done is *Reinventing Government: How the Entrepreneurial Spirit Is Transforming the Public Sector* (Addison-Wesley Publishing Company, Reading, Mass., 1992), by David Osborne and Ted Gaebler. They studied the way in which some government departments in the U.S. were changing their ways of doing business and wrote:

> We last "reinvented" our governments during the early decades of the twentieth century, roughly from 1900 through 1940. We did so ... to cope with the emergence of a new industrial economy which created vast new problems and vast new opportunities in American life. Today the world of government is once again in great flux. The emergence of a post-industrial, knowledge-based, global economy has undermined old realities throughout the world, creating wonderful opportunities and frightening problems. Governments large and small, American and foreign, federal, state, and local, have begun to respond.

Osborne and Gaebler set out ten principles that should guide government. Here we can only summarize their ideas. Governments should:

1 "Steer rather than row." That is to say, they should set policy, deliver funds, and evaluate performance rather than operate programs.
2 Empower communities by giving them ownership of public programs instead of treating them as clients to be serviced by the bureaucracy.
3 Introduce competition into delivery of public services, requiring existing government departments and private companies to bid on contracts.
4 Be driven by a mission clearly defined, and not by rules, regulations, and budgets so detailed that they control the organization.

5 Be results-oriented, which means funding the output of programs rather than the inputs. For example, instead of funding schools on the basis of how many students enrol, fund on how many students they graduate at what level.

6 Be customer- rather than bureaucracy-driven – meeting the needs of the public rather than of the civil servants.

7 Be enterprising and harness the power of the profit motive, looking at problems as an opportunity to find solutions that make money instead of just costing money.

8 Anticipate and prevent problems, instead of finding cures after the problem has emerged.

9 Decentralize management, with hierarchy of authority giving way to participation and team work.

10 Structure markets to achieve public ends. For example, instead of introducing a program to collect bottles for recycling, legislate a deposit on bottles so that it is profitable for others to collect and return them.

Governments in Canada, as in the United States, have already adopted some of these principles. For example, programs for native peoples are increasingly "owned" and administered by native community organizations. The Canadian International Development Agency discovered years ago that working through non-governmental organizations (NGOs) was often the best way to deliver aid to communities in developing countries. The federal government retained the power to regulate air traffic but got out of the business of operating an airline when it "privatized" Air Canada, selling it to private investors more likely than civil servants to keep a close eye on efficiency and profitability. In many cities garbage is collected by private contractors who bid against each other for the municipal contract. Instead of building and operating public housing, governments assist community co-operatives to do the job. While providing facilities for recreation and sports, governments increasingly offset the cost by charging a fee to those who use them. The goal is not to cut back on public services but to provide them in a more economical manner, so that cuts are less likely to be required by budgetary constraints.

But the advantage of this new style of government is not merely economy. When community organizations rather than bureaucrats take responsibility for managing programs introduced by governments to solve public problems, it is a form of participatory democracy. Much more could be done because developed democracies seem to be producing growing numbers of non-governmental organizations of volunteer workers, which undertake all manner of projects. Many are charitable – for example, food banks. Some are educational – for example, those promoting literacy. Others are organized around causes such as preserving the environment or aiding development abroad. Think of an issue in social reform and community development, and there will be at least one NGO working on it. They mobilize concerned citizens, with energy, education and/or skills, who are prepared to donate part of their leisure time to tackling social problems. Why not hand over schools to NGOs made up of parents, teachers, and pupils? Perhaps community NGOs would be better than civil servants at assessing need and administering public welfare, and so on.

The greatest opposition would probably come from public service unions. They exist to protect the jobs and working conditions of their civil servant members, and fiercely resist any attempt to downsize government or to transfer work from the bureaucracy to the more competitive private sector. While their primary motive is the welfare of their members, they often support parties which claim to be social democratic. The argument seems to be that to preserve big government is to preserve social democracy, but this is a fundamental error. Social democracy depends not on big government but on good government which enjoys public respect because it is efficient, economical, and responsive to public need. Policies which produce that sort of government are social democratic; resistance to such policies is reactionary.

SUPPORT FOR FUNDAMENTAL CHANGE?

It is commonly said that Canadians are fed up with talk about the constitution, and that by rejecting the Charlottetown accord they instructed their politicians to focus on more immediate problems, such as the economy. Prime Minister Chrétien goes so far as to say that there can be no more talk of constitutional reform for at least twenty-five years, and some provincial premiers agree. On the other hand, the western provinces were demanding until quite recently that they be given a louder voice in a much more powerful Senate, and both the Citizens' Forum and the 1993 federal election suggested a widespread desire for reform of politics generally.

The populist Reform party, for example, won support while proposing to modify what is now a system of representative democracy to include elements of direct democracy. Under the Reform plan, MPs would not be elected to do as they and their party thought best in the national interest. On some issues they would be expected to vote as instructed by their constituents. If they displeased a majority of their constituents, they could be recalled and replaced. In short, they would to some extent be delegates rather than representatives. And going further, major issues might be taken out of the hands of the Commons and submitted to the people in referendums. Such a system would no longer be "responsible government," as we call our system – that is, government responsible to the House of Commons, which appoints and may dismiss it.

Nor would Reform's proposed structure be parliamentary in the customary sense, yet it appealed to many Canadians fed up with the existing system, particularly in the West.

Québécois voted strongly for another new party, the Bloc Québécois, which promised not merely to reform the political system, but to scrap Confederation and seek a new deal between an independent Quebec and the rest of Canada. The initial appeal of Prime Minister Kim Campbell was precisely that she was new and promised to do politics in a new way. Sensing the desire for change in the system of elite decision-making, she promised a more open and inclusionary style, although what she had in mind was never made clear. The Liberal leader and winner, Jean Chrétien, was a veteran of the old politics, but nevertheless struck a new note by publishing at the outset of the campaign a detailed program and promising that he would be accountable to the voters for implementing every word of it – a rash commitment and inconsistent with the principle that government is responsible to the Commons and not to the public at large.

Therefore, it may be correct to say that Canadians are no longer interested in *talking* about fundamental constitutional change, but only in the sense that they are fed up with talking and want to do something serious about it. They may indeed want to focus on economic problems, but they are sensible enough to know that the two go hand in hand. Government manages the economy, and government in a state of confusion, constantly at war with itself, unable to command majority support in a divided country, is unlikely to manage efficiently on a daily basis. It is even less likely to deal successfully with the basic challenges posed by globalization.

Canadians also know that Quebec's discontents will not simply vanish from the national agenda. For many years there has been substantial support among Québécois for some form of separatism. The recent election of the Parti Québécois government ensures that the constitutional debate will resume and lead to a referendum in Quebec on separation. The question is whether to await Quebec's initiative and then perhaps be forced to accept the division of the country in a mood of failure and bitterness, or to recognize that our federal and political systems are failing us all, not Quebec alone, and that we all – English and French, easterners, westerners, and those in between – should undertake a fundamental review of our Confederation.

Every opinion poll in Quebec shows a majority would prefer a reorganized Canada to separation. And a poll commissioned by *Maclean's* magazine and published 1 July 1994 found a surprising level of national support for decentralization. Sixty-four percent of Canadians outside of Quebec favoured transfer of significant powers from Ottawa to the provinces; and 66 percent would agree to giving all provinces the same deal as sought by Quebec.

Offered the opportunity and the tools to reinvent their future, to design a form of government more open to popular participation, more efficient in managing affairs, and much less costly, Canadians would probably respond with enthusiasm.

HOW DO WE MAKE IT HAPPEN?

Confederation became possible when the leader of the Liberal opposition in the Canada of 1864 – the union of Ontario and Quebec – did the unexpected and offered to enter a coalition with the Conservatives to invent a new Canada. It would be equally unexpected, but also both statesmanlike and good politics, if Prime Minister Chrétien rose in the Commons one day soon and said something like:

It is clear that there is substantial demand – particularly in the West and in Quebec, but probably in other regions also – for fundamental change in our system of government. The Official Opposition in this House is committed to the sovereignty of Quebec, which would mean the end of Canada as we know it, and the third party seeks major changes in our parliamentary form of government. The first priority of this government is economic reform and progress, but we wish to respond constructively to those Canadians who believe that it is necessary also to reform our institutions of government.

We first recognized the demand for fundamental change in the 1960s when Ontario hosted a conference of provinces on the subject of "Confederation for Tomorrow" and Prime Minister Lester Pearson responded by holding the first of a series of federal-provincial conferences on the constitution. The eleven governments have since made repeated efforts to reform our system. We have had some success, notably with the adoption of the Charter of Rights and Freedoms, but the efforts of previous governments to adjust the balance of powers between the federal and provincial governments have failed. When the governments finally reached the consensus on the Charlottetown agreement, the people rejected it. I will be frank and say that as a government we would be happy to hear no more about the constitution for twenty-five years. The election of the Parti Québécois government in Quebec precludes this course, and the government wishes to initiate a national debate on our national future.

Governments have failed to find a national consensus, and now in fact have other priorities. So we propose to turn the issue back to the people. A dialogue began when the previous government appointed the independent Citizens' Forum on Canada's Future. As the Forum's commissioners recommended, we are now proposing to enrich the dialogue, and perhaps bring it toward conclusions. I am therefore inviting major non-governmental organizations representing business and labour, the professions, universities, cultural and ethnic groups to nominate members of a National Commission on Confederation. The task of this commission will not — I repeat not — be to suggest solutions to our problems, but to organize the widest possible public debate — a genuine people's debate in which every Canadian who wishes to participate will be able to do so, as an individual or through an organization of which he or she may be a member.

It's not for me to tell the commission how to do its work, but I hope it will seek answers to such basic questions as:

- Do we need to reform Confederation, or is it best to proceed as we are?
- If we need to make changes, should we seek to centralize or decentralize government?
- Are we satisfied with our parliamentary system of representative democracy? If not, what alternative would be preferable?

I recognize that if debate is to be responsible it will have to be informed and carefully structured, probably over a period of years rather than months. Expert analysis of the options will be required. If at the end of the debate the commission so recommends, the government will organize a plebiscite in which the people can express their opinions on fundamental questions facing Canada. An informed electorate might then wish to establish a constitutional convention.

It is our opinion that the government should remove itself as far as possible from the debate. Accordingly, and in keeping with what I believe to be the spirit of the times, members of the Commission will serve without pay and their expenses will be met by the organizations nominating them. The Commission is bound to incur some administrative expenses which the government will meet, but any major projects — for example, commissioning and publishing background material to facilitate debate — should be on a cost-recovery basis.

Initiating this national debate will, I believe, achieve two purposes. It will put national renewal on the public agenda in a constructive way, and it will remove the subject from the parliamentary agenda while we focus on the economy. It also offers the people of Quebec a choice between separatism and unreformed federalism. As the economy improves, public discontent may decrease and the national debate may find no majority on the need for fundamental change. Or we may find that the division between Quebec and the rest of Canada is so deep that it cannot be bridged by change acceptable to the majority, but in that unhappy case we shall be better prepared to negotiate a form of separation.

To recall the words of the previous Forum: "The crafters of a new federation, like the Fathers of the original one, will be called on to be bold, imaginative, and determined to let nothing stand in the way of a responsible, honourable compromise acceptable to all the federation's members."

I invite the provinces and territories, whose interest in these matters is certainly as great as that of this government, to aid us in this enterprise.

But what if the prime minister does not see the wisdom of launching a national debate? Quebec may force it upon us at some stage by voting for sovereignty, and that would be the worst of circumstances. Although the Parti Québécois and its partner in Parliament, the Bloc Québécois, insist that the rest of Canada would have no choice but to negotiate the details of separation, there would certainly be in the other provinces much anger and strong anti-Quebec sentiment. "No truck or trade with the Frenchies" would have powerful support, and it is hard to see a civilized and sensible outcome in such a divorce. Civil war is unthinkable, but hot heads on both sides might well produce local violence, making conciliation and responsible negotiations even more difficult than they would be in the best of circumstances.

As we have seen above, there are good reasons quite apart from Quebec to consider revising the Canadian union before a crisis occurs, and while a spirit of goodwill and cooperation remains.

Each of the opposition parties has reason to support a sincere attempt to reinvent Canada. The Bloc Québécois supports separation and sovereignty, but anticipates negotiations with the rest of Canada, which could result in a Canadian common market or union. The Conservative party under a Quebec leader, Jean Charest, and in search of new policies that distinguish it from the Liberals, may like the idea of boldly rebuilding the Canadian Confederation which it was largely responsible for creating in 1867. It would be an opportunity to build again the old alliance of conservative nationalists in Quebec and in English-speaking Canada. If the New Democratic Party is to survive, it has to redefine social democracy in Canada and regain from Reform its role as the voice of protest and radical change. Reinventing our system of government would surely be a good place to start. Reform so far has been unwilling to contemplate a Canada in which Quebec would not be a province just like the others, but could Reformers refuse to debate proposals for real change, which would downsize government and decentralize authority?

Then of course there are the provinces. Acting together they could probably force the hand of the federal government, as they did in 1967 when they held the "Confederation for Tomorrow" conference without federal participation. Or they could themselves organize a national debate. For that matter, a single major province could certainly raise a national storm and probably nudge Ottawa into action by announcing that it shared some of Quebec's dissatisfactions, and that if no reform was in prospect it would seek for itself a new relationship with the rest of Canada. There is already in the West, particularly in British Columbia, an inclination to think the region gains little from Confederation and might in fact be better off in a much looser union. Even Ontario is now beginning to complain that it can no longer afford to finance the less developed provinces, and to call for a new deal with Ottawa.

The price of doing nothing will be a continued drift into disarray, and possibly a financial storm while Quebec makes up its mind and in so doing determines the future for the rest of us. Even if Quebec once again elects to remain in Confederation, imbalances will remain, and we shall still have a dysfunctional federalism and an undemocratic parliament, both of which weaken our economy. How much better it would be to take charge of our own future before crisis is upon us.

POSTSCRIPT

And now, returning to Hegel, where does the crisis of social democracy leave the dialectic? The U.S. thinker and writer Francis Fukuyama excited world-wide interest in 1989 with a provocative article in *The National Interest,* a small but influential U.S. review, in which he suggested that the defeat of Soviet communism marked the end of the dialectic because no new ideology had arisen to challenge the victorious "democratic egalitarianism" – liberal democracy in the political sphere and capitalism in the economic. He later elaborated his arguments in a book, *The End of History and the Last Man* (The Free Press, New York, 1992). He was not, as some critics imagined, announcing the end of war, famine, disease, and other disasters that we treat as milestones of history, but the end of the evolution of consciousness and social organization.

Nor was he a simple-minded right-winger celebrating the victory of capitalism over communism. In fact, he thought a future without ideological conflict might be horribly dull, and he saw the possibility that without a just cause for which to struggle bored humanity might choose an unjust cause. Although we like to pretend that we are all lovers of peace and tranquillity, war – as he pointed out – has often been a popular public diversion, an escape from routine and what is normally thought of as good behaviour into a world of risk and adventure.

It may be, as Fukuyama suggests, that the best we can hope for in the future is to fine-tune liberal democracy, as he called our system. But in my view, the dialectic has at least one more stage before we reach the end, and the clash of systems is already evident. The central goal of all the ideologies we have been discussing – capitalism, socialism, and social democracy – is endless economic growth, but that goal is now being challenged on the grounds that the world's environment cannot support much more growth, and that in any event the consumer society is not the good society for which we strive. Once on the fringe of politics, environmentalists are now in the mainstream. Governments everywhere acknowledge that pollution is a critical problem, but they cannot yet imagine a world without growth. They are therefore promoting sustainable development – the idea that with the right policies and technologies we can have both economic growth and a healthy environment.

It is certainly true that we could do much more than we are to limit damage to the environment, particularly in the developing countries racing to catch up with industrial development in the West and understandably unwilling to accept limits to growth. But the notion that economic growth can continue for ever is implausible. Shopping has become a recreation rather than a search for necessities for millions of people in the developed democracies, and stores are already piled high with more consumer goods than they can sell. The conventional economic wisdom was that demand produced supply: when government put money into the pockets of consumers, they demanded more goods and services, business increased the supply, and the economy grew. But when consumer tastes are jaded and appetites sated, it is the supply of new conveniences, amusements, and luxuries that creates demand. For example, consumers with money to spend did not demand VCRs and microwave ovens, but when those products were invented and marketed, consumers rushed to buy, new industries were created, and the economy expanded.

But for how long will this sort of growth continue? Given that production depletes resources and almost inevitably creates pollution, how long should it continue? Although advertising tirelessly spreads the gospel that to spend is to be happy, there appears to be a revival of interest in spiritual – that is, non-material – values. Books on how to improve the quality of our lives are high on every bestseller list. The dialectical struggle of the coming century, therefore, is likely to be between the thesis of economic growth to produce ever rising standards of material wealth, and the antithesis of a society that is content with its material condition and seeks spiritual and intellectual enrichment. The synthesis might look very much like socialism, even communism. But it is not yet practical politics and in the meantime we have to deal with the situation as it is. As we cannot return to laissez-faire capitalism, that means making social democracy work better until the dialectic produces a superior model.